CHRISTIANITY RUBS HOLES IN MY RELIGION

by Bob Murphy

published by
Hunter Ministries Publishing Company
1600 Townhurst
Houston, Texas 77043

©Copyright 1976 by Bob Murphy, all rights reserved. Published by Hunter Ministries Publishing Company, 1600 Townhurst, Houston, Texas 77043. Printed in U.S.A.

Scripture quotations are taken from:

The Authorized King James Version (KJV)
The Living Bible, Copyright 1971, by the Tyndale House Publishers, Wheaton, Illinois 60187. Used by permission.
Unless otherwise indicated, KJV is used.

Dedicated to Charles and Frances Hunter and the excitement of the adventure in Christ!

A collection of short essays on growing and learning in the Christian adventure. The experiences are mine and need not necessarily be yours. But I share in love some of what has happened in my life...

Bob Murphy

April 1976

FOREWORD

Bob Murphy is the most delightful drunk in the world! And he's constantly in that state! Whether it's late at night, or early in the morning, he's always high, but in a different way than he used to be. What he's been imbibing for a decade is the best wine in the world, because it's the NEW wine! It's the wine that *can* and *does* change lives, even of people who never were alcoholics.

This book will speak to every person in the world! In one way or another, it will touch you, and might even prick you in a way you don't like, but it will do so in a way to make YOU want to change your life style, whether it's drinking, eating or criticizing those who do.

Or maybe you've got a little extra dose of "religion." This book takes care of that too, in one of the funniest ways we've ever seen. For those Sunday Christians who display their Christianity in splendid trappings on Sunday and then put it back in the vault until the next Sunday, Bob Murphy really has something to say that's worth listening to. He believes it is a "bubbling and exciting experience seven days a week, anywhere and everywhere I go" and we can't help but agree with him.

He might even speak to you like he spoke to us. As we were reading the manuscript, we came to the chapter about the people who are always slapping you on the back, and shaking your hand and saying "You're doing a wonderful job, Bob, I sure couldn't do it! Keep up the good work!" but who never put their money where their mouth is. We had seen the work he was doing and constantly congratulated him for what he was accomplishing, but never realized that God was calling on us to help him provide the food for the people whose lives had been so greatly influenced by him. God provides, but God provides THROUGH people many times.

The funny thing about the book is that you may think you don't have a single problem, but it will reveal to you in the sneakiest way something you didn't even realize was a problem, and give you the answer!

You might have to get used to his unique style of writing. Like a breathless child holding to his father's hand, who never finishes a sentence, his short little choppy phrases reflect the excitement he has found in the real way to stay drunk - on the Holy Spirit! He lives it every single moment of every day and night. You'll never forget what this book has to say!

Charles ♡♡ Frances Hunter

Ephesians 6:13-18 (TLB) "So use every piece of God's armor to resist the enemy whenever he attacks, and when it is all over, you will still be standing up.

"But to do this, you will need the strong belt of truth and the breastplate of God's approval.

"Wear shoes that are able to speed you on as you preach the Good News of peace with God.

"In every battle you will need faith as your shield to stop the fiery arrows aimed at you by Satan.

"And you will need the helmet of salvation and the sword of the Spirit - which is the Word of God.

"Pray all the time. Ask God for anything in line with the Holy Spirit's wishes. Plead with him, reminding him of your needs, and keep praying earnestly for all Christians everywhere."

PRELUDE: MILK VS MEAT

In editing this material we found some of the words too strong, so we took them out; others we removed, only to put them back in the finished manuscript.

St. Paul in a letter to the Church at Corinth said, "I have fed you with milk, and not with meat: for hitherto ye were not able to bear it, neither yet now are ye able." (I Cor. 3:2)

I do hope I have given a balanced meal of milk and meat in this writing. These things I share are what I have learned, and what I am still learning.

Paul spoke of "babes in Christ" in this same writing, and I often wonder if we don't remain in the "spiritual nursery" too long - if we aren't still crawling Christians when we should be walking or running in the adventure of living for Christ! By the power of the Holy Spirit we can and should grow up and get with it in our lives and in our witness for the Lord.

If my personality shows in this book, bear in mind that God does not change our basic personalities when we become Christians. He just rearranges them to suit his own purpose for our good and for his glory. I stopped trying to be someone else with his Christian style long ago. I am trying to be the best possible Christian, my style, for today!

If you are amused by my experience, do have a good laugh in the Lord! Christian laughter never hurt anyone and it would do a lot of good for many of us. If you are shocked, go read Psalm 23. It's always a good balm for shock, Christian or otherwise, and if you are inspired to new action and new depths of Christian experience, then my purpose in sharing will be fulfilled.

My work is with alcoholics. In this area of work we cannot afford to be vague or terribly polite. We must be blunt and direct because the alternatives to recovery are insanity and death.

Recently I was wondering if I shouldn't be softer and more sedate in writing or talking to fellow Christians. Consider the alternatives of Christianity and sin: Heaven or hell, joy or sorrow, peace or pressure, deliverance or destruction, healing or pain, delight or depression. ARE THE ALTERNATIVES REALLY ANY DIFFERENT than life versus insanity and death for an alcoholic?

You be yourself, and I'll be myself, but let's walk together to find the difference between vital Christianity and mere religion!

TABLE OF CONTENTS

LET'S VISIT FOR A SPELL 13
A BRIEF LOOK BACKWARD 14
THE YEARS IN-BETWEEN 17
THE BEGINNING OF LIGHT 21
A NEW EXPERIENCE 25
ANOTHER KIND OF DRUNK! 27
OLD GOSPELS AND NEW MEANINGS 29
THE OPENING OF NEW DOORS.................31
SOME RAIN AND SOME RAINBOWS.............34
SOME OF THE ODDS AND ENDS.................38
TO BE IN THE WORLD,
  BUT NOT OF THE WORLD....................40
THE GIFT OF EXPERIENCE 44
RELIGION IS OFTEN BIG BUSINESS,
  CHRISTIANITY IS NOT 47
REQUESTS AND DELIVERIES 49
SILK PURSES MADE FROM SOW'S EARS!........56
THE GREATEST OF THESE IS LOVE! 58
GODLY INDIVIDUALITY.........................60
ON JOINING A CHURCH 63
ENCOUNTER WITH AN OLD FRIEND 66
MEETING EXCITED CHRISTIANS! 68
ABOUT WATER BAPTISM 70
ABOUT DELIVERANCE 72
A SPIRITUAL ILLNESS 75
THE VALLEY OF THE SHADOW OF FAT! 77
THE FRUIT EXPERTS 79
GOD HAS A SENSE OF HUMOR 80
SOCIAL OUTREACH 82
THE CHARISMATIC MOVEMENT 86
A MORE EXCELLENT WAY 88

BOOM BOOM RAZZMATAZZ
  RELIGION! 92
DIGNITY WITH POWER.........................95
A LITTLE AND A LOT 96
INVOLVEMENT—JESUS' STYLE 99
GOD'S MOVING COMPANY 103
WHY SERENITY FARM, INC.? 105
LUNCH WITH A MIRACLE 109
THE "TESTIMONY MEETING" 112

CHAPTER I
LET'S VISIT FOR A SPELL

As we visit and I share some of what I have learned and experienced, I do not pretend for a minute that I have all the answers for myself or for you. Be wary of anyone who tells you he has all the answers. We all still see through a glass darkly, and we know in part. (I Cor. 13:12) But we can all share in our love and experience and lift one another up.

The rich adventure of Christianity is like a school. We are all students. We are not all in the same grade at the same time. Some of the older students can be a great help to some of the newer ones. Some of the greatest restatements of God's truth have come to me out of the mouths of new people fresh in the excitement of the Lord.

Many of us have wandered around for years without any real purpose or meaning in our lives. We clothed ourselves in the cloak of religion until we found that it left us sadly lacking in our lives. It is when we experience the living reality of Jesus Christ that we put on the "whole armour of God." When we do this, we find that it will often not fit over the cloak of religion and begins to wear holes in it. Deeper spiritual meanings and shallow religious exercises do not fit together very well. Many new experiences and real adjustments come about as we begin the adventure of "reality" Christianity!

Come with me!

CHAPTER 2

A BRIEF LOOK BACKWARD

Lot's wife looked back, and she turned to a pillar of salt, so I have not often allowed myself the practice of looking back. To appreciate what I know today, I must look back for a bit at what I once believed to be truth. I can never truly be grateful for what I am until I look back at what I once was. Let's take a look at what the Lord had to work with - it wasn't much!

My father was a minister in a fundamentalist church. Because of this, my heart always goes out to the children of ministers. Some of us must overcome our knowledge of the mechanics of religion to find the truth of Christianity. It is rather like being the child of an actor in the theater. If you've grown up backstage you can never really enjoy a performance because you know all the techniques which create the illusions. CHRISTIANITY IS VERY REAL. Much of religion is not! To be able to separate the two is an act of God in his love and mercy.

Our church had a strange doctrine, a sort of do-it-yourself religion with some strange rules and side effects. The experience of salvation was a trip down to an altar, or the "mourner's bench," in front of the congregation. It was an emotional binge full of tears of repentance. The more emotion one displayed, the more "saved" he was. Persons with emotional control were thought to be less sincere and less apt to reach a saved state. Sermons aimed at enticing you down to the front were full of emotionalism and fear. The fear of hellfire and damnation was quite effective in days before air-conditioning.

I usually got saved twice each year, once in the summer revival and again in the winter revival. Sometimes, if a weekend preacher was especially dramatic in his descriptions of the fires of hell, I would be saved a third or fourth time. These salvation experiences, charged with emotion and fear, were never lasting. It seemed as if the evangelist packed up my salvation in his suitcase and took it on with him to the next place. Because these preachers were lifting up hellfire and fear as a reason for salvation, it was not a valid experience.

Jesus said, "And I, IF I BE LIFTED UP FROM THE EARTH, WILL DRAW ALL MEN UNTO ME." (John 12:32) He did not say that lifting up fear of hell or punishment would do a thing for us. It was years later that I finally knew that the love of Jesus Christ gives PERFECT PEACE AND FREEDOM FROM ALL FEAR!

After salvation, one began a real do-it-yourself chore. One must begin to discipline himself to the church standards and doctrines and give up bad habits and worldly pleasures by pulling himself up by his own spiritual bootstraps. Folks quit smoking, quit drinking, quit dancing, playing cards, and a long list of other things that "church Christians" did not do. Women were expected to have long hair worn simply in a bun at the back of the head. No makeup of any kind except powder, no jewelry, no low-cut dresses or any kind of fancy adornment was allowed!

I used to look at all these plain people who were to live in heaven after death, and I decided that with such terribly plain-looking citizens, heaven really needed those streets of gold and pearly gates to jazz it up a bit. I found it difficult to imagine spending all eternity with such a plain lot. As a child I often wondered if the hereafter wouldn't really be an awful bore, and whether or not these plain people could actually play harps of gold and sing out eternal praises to God. Some of the ideas people have on what makes them acceptable to our Lord still amaze me!

Those were bitter years filled with confused thoughts. I tried to look as plain as possible. I tried not reading the Sunday newspaper on Sunday. I went to church because my family required it. The more I tried, the more confused I became. I could not, by my own efforts, be anything. NOBODY TOLD ME IT WAS GRACE, AND NOT WORKS, WHICH GAVE ME WHAT I SOUGHT!

These were good people, sincere people. Later I came to the realization that goodness and sincerity are not nearly enough. People who burned witches in Salem were quite sincere. A mother who kills her child in a pagan sacrifice is more than sincere, and these sincere people turned me off completely. By the time I was twelve I had come to the conclusion that I would not get into heaven because it was impossible for me. I decided that I'd live my life as best I could with the knowledge that hell waited for me at the end of it. I knew I could never make it with the do-it-yourself program presented to me.

It was many years later before I read those wonderful words of our Lord, "WITH MEN THIS IS IMPOSSIBLE; BUT WITH GOD ALL THINGS ARE POSSIBLE." (Matt. 19:26)

CHAPTER 3

THE YEARS IN-BETWEEN

I once read, "There are no wasted years, there are only years of soul education." I like that thought! I believe it! David wrote, "I can never be lost to your Spirit! I can never get away from my God! If I go up to heaven, you are there; if I go down to the place of the dead, you are there. If I ride the morning winds to the farthest oceans, even there your hand will guide me, your strength will support me. If I try to hide in the darkness, the night becomes light around me. For even darkness cannot hide from God; to you the night shines as bright as day. Darkness and light are both alike to you." (Psalm 139: 7-12 TLB) We can't run off somewhere and get away from God. We may spend many years unaware of his presence, but he is always near and ready for us to turn to him.

The years I spent living it up in a mad whirl of career, success, money, liquor, and all the other so-called trimmings were really years of learning. (But this is the type of learning experience that I do not recommend.) Now when I read, "Seek ye first the kingdom of God, and his righteousness..." (Matt. 6:33) I know the TRUTH of it from my own experience as well as from the light of the Holy Spirit and scriptural discernment. There is nothing else to try! I have already had a fling at most all of it. It did not bring either happiness or peace of mind. I am certain I knew this long before I was ready to admit it in my conscious mind.

I traveled and did everything I wanted to do. I drank to dull the loneliness of it all, but the alcohol only created more loneliness. There began a merry-go-round of existence which lasted far too long, because I really didn't know how to get off. It never stopped long enough for me to try to get off.

I knew fascinating people. I lived in fantastic places and made an excellent income in the music and entertainment world, but the more I sought happiness and peace, the farther it seemed from my world. I knew at the age of twenty-three that I did not drink liquor like other people. I knew that I drank earlier than they did and that I drank more. I needed more to keep up the pace. I knew then that one day alcohol would be a problem for me if I didn't learn some control. Where or how one learned to control drinking alcohol I did not know.

While I was familiar with the word "bum," I never heard the word "alcoholic." I did not know that some people have a three-fold sickness and addiction which is spiritual, physical, and mental. It is difficult when you are young and successful to admit that you have a problem; certainly it is difficult to take action on a problem of this nature. All the tomorrows that loom ahead seem like ample time to face whatever serious corrections are needed. I continued a pace that was much too fast because I didn't know how to stop.

To relate all that happened to this once totally lost soul is neither desirable nor an effective witness. Jesus did not tell us to lift up our sin experience. We are to lift up Jesus and then he can draw all men unto himself. Let's skip the miserable details of the many years I was learning from a negative way all the things which do not bring peace of mind and soul. A few times I tried to reach out to God again, but my image of God was still that he was angry and vindictive. Nobody had told me with any conviction that God is love. It is not possible to reach out toward a God of hate and revenge. I was already full of guilt and remorse. I needed no God of wrath to make it worse.

The last thing I needed was for some religionist to tell me just how rotten I was. I already knew this from the bottom of my very soul. I knew no loving Christians.

Those I had known and suspected of having love were far distant. I did not want to take a chance on the disappointment of finding out that they too did not have any real love. So the lonely years and the treatment of myself with alcohol continued.

Please never judge an alcoholic! When you see him, do pray for him. While you cannot possibly understand him, do not condemn or lecture. Speak to him with love, because he is actually starving for love and understanding. As you go on your way, commit him to the care of a loving God, because that is the only real answer for alcoholism. Never tell him how bad he is or how good he could or should be. Nobody knows this better than he does. He seeks just that. Too often he continues to seek in the wrong way. Only a real and personal spiritual recovery will begin a lasting and peaceful recovery from this most horrible addictive illness.

I do not know when I became an alcoholic. There is no date and no deadline. Nobody knows when he crosses that line between a social drinking situation and the line where he is hooked. From all that is known, once you have crossed over, you can never again return to controlled or social drinking.

I know our Lord turned water into wine at a wedding party. I know that bread and wine were served at The Last Supper. I assume from scripture that our Lord drank some wine with meals as was the custom of his time on earth. Possibly our Lord did, but I have a chemical imbalance and I cannot drink wine or any other spirits.

Our Lord also walked on water. I can't!

St. Paul said, "Use a little wine for thy stomach's sake." (I Tim. 5:23) This statement has been a stumbling block for many alcoholics who read into the scriptures a blessing on their drinking, but end with a curse on their life. I'm sure St. Paul will not mind if I skip the wine. My stomach is doing very well these days due to God's miracle! Certainly Paul would not encourage destruction. To an alcoholic a little is a lot.

I became an alcoholic and did nothing about it until I was thirty-nine years old.

CHAPTER 4
THE BEGINNING OF LIGHT

By the time I was thirty-nine I was a complete and total mess! I had tried it all, and nothing worked.

How many there are who, when there is no place else to turn and they've tried everything else, finally turn to God. That was me! How sad that we dash ourselves to pieces before we turn to him and allow him to put the pieces back together again. What needless and senseless pain we inflict upon ourselves! From the bottom, there is no place to go but up; however, a one-way adventure going upward is not a bad idea when you can't go anyplace else.

I located a fellowship of men and women who offered me a "GOD AS I UNDERSTOOD HIM." This was the first time in my life that anyone had allowed me a personal and individual idea of God. Always before, it had been someone else's angry God who was just itching to send us all to hell anyway. Someone told me, "God isn't mad at you, and he will help you."

My opening bargain with God was that he allow me freedom from alcoholism. Nothing more I asked. I did not ask to be saved because I thought I was beyond salvation. I did not ask to go to heaven instead of hell because I knew I wasn't worthy. I read material on spiritual recovery from alcoholism. I asked questions. I got direct answers because these people in the fellowship were all alcoholics and they deal in the direct answer. They cannot afford to do otherwise.

I WISH MORE CHRISTIANS HAD DIRECT ANSWERS FOR DIRECT QUESTIONS so that we knew where we stood. I wish that more Christians would state their beliefs in simple and direct terms, or that we had the honesty to say, "I do not know," when, in fact, we don't have all the answers. It took me many years to learn that Christianity does not confer an instant, complete education on us and we can say, "I don't know," and still be effective.

With the fellowship of people who understood me because they had been where I was, things began to happen. I got down on my knees by my bed and prayed, asking God to remove the desire to drink liquor, because I knew that I would never make it without the removal of that desire. I told God this in no uncertain terms. There was no flash of light and no great spiritual experience, but sometime between the time I stopped drinking and three months later I lost all desire for drinking. In all the years since then, I have been around alcohol in almost every form in connection with my work. Never once have I been tempted to drink!

This was my first introduction to a miracle from God just for the asking. Quietly and surely, without fanfare, God had given me freedom from an addiction which can kill you. I reasoned that if God could and would do this without any great effort on my part, perhaps he would do other things, and that my earlier experience of do-it-yourself religion might have been wrong.

I began to read the Bible for myself and to ask for guidance in learning for my personal use what I needed to know. As I prayed for various needs, I received them. INDEED, GOD WAS NOT MAD AT ME! I could ask and receive! I met some wonderful women with the light of Christ's freedom shining in their faces even though they wore lipstick! Some even had very attractive clothes and necklines! Some of the men were far from perfect and did not pretend to be, but oh, the excellent witness to deliverance and peace!

I began to learn, but some of the old teaching haunted me and because I had such a good and personal thing going with the Lord, I didn't dare go near a church. I was so afraid they might mess it all up with rules and regulations.

My time continued with just the Lord and me and the wonderful privacy of my initial growing and learning. I began to understand THE REAL NECESSITY OF LOVING AND FORGIVING. For the first time in my life I knew the meaning of The Lord's Prayer and understood that we ask to be forgiven as we forgive. I thought that if the Lord put this condition into my own relationship with him, I'd better get busy and ask him to help me forgive those folks I felt were unforgivable. I included in this list my late parents and those plain folks in the church where I received my earlier training. They could not pass on to me something that they did not have. They only gave what had been given to them. With this revelation, I found the joy and peace of real forgiveness.

Within this framework of clearing away the wreckage of my own past, I asked God to forgive my past sins. Then I was able to forgive myself for those deeds which could not be undone. This is clearing away the haunting guilt of things past in the most basic way, and I do heartily recommend it to any new Christian. As the Lord forgives you of your past, FORGIVE YOURSELF, and do not allow the self-punishment and guilt to remain in your mind.

Salvation was through the atonement provided by Jesus Christ and not by the length of a lady's hair or her lipstick! It was not some awful and impossible do-it-yourself program that made me "worthy." I could get to heaven, not by my own merits, but simply by accepting what Jesus Christ had already done for me two thousand years ago. What a simple way, so easily understood. Why had it been so COMPLICATED by men who presented a God of wrath and a set of traditions impossible to follow?

My initial experience with Jesus was literally coming from darkness into light! I have always felt a bit sorry for those "lifetime career Christians," those who grew up in such "spiritual" ways that they never knew darkness. I do not suggest that you go out and experience great sin in order to appreciate great salvation. I do state, however, that those of us who have known the darkness of night truly feel and appreciate the wonder of daylight!

In this time of being fed with God's milk of kindness and compassion, I learned to KEEP MY CHRISTIANITY SIMPLE. Later, as I began to partake of the meat of the Word and grow in scriptural understanding, I learned to often GO BACK TO THAT SAME SIMPLICITY. "Ask, and it shall be given you; seek, and ye shall find; knock, and it shall be opened unto you." (Luke II:9) Such a new and wonderful way to live, especially when you have come to life from a half-dead state of alcoholism!

I began to study the Bible and because I passed on the word that God isn't mad at us, I became known as a "kook" or at best a spiritual nut. I was often called "Father Murphy," and such statements as, "Here comes Billy Graham," would hit my ears. These statements would have sent me into an Irish trauma and total anger a few years before. Now I felt that such a statement meant that I was in pretty good company and on the right track. When you've been called some of the things an active alcoholic is called, "Billy Graham" isn't so bad! I had heard Billy Graham, and we believed the same things and talked about the same things. So who cared what they called me! Besides, with such publicity, I found new areas to witness. My phone often rang at 3 A.M. with someone wanting to know if God really did answer prayer and change big problems. THE ANSWER IS AND WAS ALWAYS, "YES!"

CHAPTER 5
A NEW EXPERIENCE

At the end of about two sober years, and into the new relationship with the Lord, I went to visit relatives in a west Texas town. During the visit I had coffee with an old drinking buddy. He wasn't an alcoholic, but we did toss off a few in our day. I shared with him my deliverance from alcoholism. To my complete surprise, he shared with me his experience with the baptism in the Holy Spirit and praying in tongues. Here was a former swinger and a few other things, talking like a "card-carrying" holy roller in the most open way.

I was fascinated.

With the power of the Holy Spirit in his witness, he made this experience seem like the next natural step in the upward spiral. No big deal and no looking down his nose at me because my experience did not include such a work; just questions and answers in a normal way! I came home from the visit with John Sherrill's book, *They Speak With Other Tongues*, and was convinced that this was not an "optional" kind of thing, but the next step in my own growth.

Not knowing anyone in my own city who had such an experience, I went back out to visit again. This time I went directly to the Sunday services at a local Pentecostal church. I thought they had the local franchise and that was the only place you could get the baptism in the Holy Spirit, but the Lord saw fit to correct my limited thinking, and nothing happened at the church. I later received this unusual experience in the home of a retired Methodist minister! This way God let me know in no uncertain terms that HIS WORKS ARE NOT FRAN-

CHISED OR COPYRIGHTED BY ANY PERSON OR GROUP.

This was not an emotional binge! I think I had expected some copy of my friend's experience, which did include emotion; however, God let me know that he deals with each of us personally and individually. GOD DOES NOT DEAL IN CHEAP CARBON COPIES. HE DEALS IN GLORIOUS ORIGINALS! My own experience in the wonder of God's individual dealings has been a great help in my years of working with other alcoholics. God does not handle any two persons alike. The gifts and experiences are available to all believing seekers, but the way we receive and the way we grow may be vastly different. I thought, like many others, that the extra gifts of our Lord were at the very end of the climb. Experience has taught me, however, that this is not true. These are the tools for living, and a means of travel, not the arrival point!

I have arrived at many spiritual plateaus only to learn that this was a resting place and that there is still a long way to travel. Life does not stand still. It moves! Christianity is no exception to God's plan of movement. *Anything which stands still stagnates.* Movement, growing, learning, and a forward motion have been my experience and my understanding. Let me say that it is often difficult, but never dull. *The greatest adventure in the world is the Christian adventure,* and just think, I, who could never bear to be bored, took so long in finding the only guarantee against boredom that this world offers! It is the walk with Jesus Christ, the never-ending amazement at the wonder of Almighty God, the limitless mercy and love which he so freely gives. Although I am not an emotional person, my eyes often fill with tears of gratitude at the wonder of it all, the liberating passport of John 3:16, "For God so loved the world, that he gave his only begotten Son, that whosoever believeth in him should not perish, but have everlasting life." No wonder we sometimes have tears of gratitude for such limitless love!

CHAPTER 6

ANOTHER KIND OF DRUNK!

So far I have discussed my alcoholism and recovery and some of the experiences encountered with the various drunks with whom we deal in our work. Now let me say a few words about a different kind of drunk.

If you will get your Bible and read the Book of Acts, you'll learn that the actions of believers on the Day of Pentecost were so far-out that the local citizenry thought they were drunk! The answer to the statement, "They're drunk," was "It's much too early for that! People don't get drunk by 9 A.M.!"

This is wonderful! Who can better understand this kind of drunk than a recovered alcoholic who has had a charismatic experience! Nothing is more bothersome to a sober person than a drunk. Nothing is more boring to a drunk than a sober person! So the next time someone in your church or parish has some new and peculiar spiritual experience, and you think they are rather odd, remember you may be dealing with a spiritual drunk. While he may bother you, you may bore him! Let's all try to deal with this in Christian love. In earthly terms, there is one simple way to deal with a bothersome drunk, GET DRUNK WITH HIM! Then he won't be any different!

If your fellow Christian who is charismatic bothers you too much, try reading the four Gospels again and the promises which they contain. Then take a few big gulps of the Book of Acts. Ask our Lord to zap you with the special and unusual blessings mentioned there. Then be prepared to get so high on the wine of the Spirit that you'll wonder how you ever managed without it. Now you can take another look at that "odd fellow" in your parish and you'll not find him too bothersome. You may get spiritually drunk together and just love it. BE CAREFUL, however, because you'll now find those other sober Christians bother and bore you. The whole process begins again as you witness.

Those spiritual drunks of two thousand years ago were not a single or isolated case. It is happening right now all over the world to people who are seeking the reality of Jesus Christ in bold new ways!

It is simply so wonderful that you'll never want to recover from this new dimension in spiritual living! Don't look for a recovery group for this kind of drunk! There isn't any! You won't desire one!

Be prepared for other folks to think you are a bit odd. Bless them. Pray for them. Witness if you are led to do so.

Oh, the joy that will flood your soul from the top of your head to the bottom of your feet! No champagne party on earth can ever equal the power of the Holy Spirit in the lives of men and women today. Talk about a HIGH! Man, you've got one! It's all in the book of Acts. Read it. Accept it, and you'll never be the same in any area of your life again!

If you happen to be one of those people with a "little" earthly alcohol problem, you can't afford to miss it! Take it from one old delivered drunk to another, "Buddy, you gotta have a taste of this!"

CHAPTER 7
OLD GOSPELS AND NEW MEANINGS

Don't look in your Bible for answers (if you aren't ready to receive them), because if you do look, you will find some. When you find them, you will then be required to take action on what you know. I was just vaguely aware of some scriptures and knew they were very nice ideas, and what a sweet world it would be if everybody lived according to such teachings.
Love your neighbor as yourself!
Wouldn't it be super swell if everyone did just that? In my new way of reading, I learned by the enlightenment of the Holy Spirit that I could not be concerned with what everyone else was doing. IF I HAD UNDERSTANDING, THEN I MUST ACT ON IT! I must *actually love* my neighbor as myself. I came to understand that this was no do-it-yourself project because I found some people most unlovable. It is only by the power of the Holy Spirit that such neighborly love is given.

I didn't *learn* to love other people. It just bubbled up from deep within me and was there. This is no gushing kind of pretend love. IT IS REAL! I AM REAL! I can be as hard as steel when it comes to the cold facts of alcoholism in my dealings with needy alcoholics. I love them enough to cut the polite pretense and give them the facts that will save their lives.

Alcoholism CAN kill you. Alcoholism WILL kill you if you don't get help. God is *the answer* and THE ONLY REAL ANSWER I KNOW ABOUT. These are cold, hard facts, but they are always given in love and with complete feeling for the questioner. Loving others then, is not an exercise in religion, but a bubbling well of the gift of our Lord. Where I couldn't love, he instilled in me the supernatural inclination to love others as myself. Loving myself after losing all self-respect was also a God-given supernatural accomplishment.

Other scriptures began to take on real meaning. The Sermon on the Mount teaches that I should not lay up treasures on earth where moth and rust corrupt and where the stock market goes up and down. It teaches that my treasure should be in heaven. Wherever my treasure is, there also is my heart and my effort and my attention (see Matt. 6:21). I had already laid up a few of this world's goodies, but I found no peace in such stored treasures. From my own experience, it was easy to see that my life should and could be free of such bounty hunting.

The Lord's Prayer says, "Give us this day our daily bread" (Matt. 6:11). It does not say, "Give me a freezer full, because I may have a party next week." It is the DAILY WALK and the DAILY NEED about which I need only be concerned.

Treasure storage went out the door, and my life began to turn upside down as I found REAL MEANING IN THE GOSPELS FOR TODAY. If I seek first the Kingdom of God and his righteousness, then whatever I need will be added as I need it. I have found this to be absolutely true. AT NO TIME HAVE I EVER BEEN WITHOUT WHATEVER I NEED. I have sometimes been lacking in WHAT I WANT, but what we WANT and what we NEED are two different things.

CHAPTER 8

THE OPENING OF NEW DOORS

Unless you really mean it, never pray, "Lord, put some use and real purpose into my life," because he will do just that! I don't even know why I decided to move out of a lovely and expensive apartment near the elegant River Oaks section. What did a single man need with a big old house in the older section of the city? I made the move and then shortly after that the Lord sort of slipped it to me very subtly. If I just took in one or two newly recovering alcoholics I might be able to do some good. With only one or two, I could still work and make a living and keep us going.

You don't just take in one or two suffering alcoholics for long. The word spreads and you have a houseful of needy people all wanting to know how you can be so happy when you used to drink two fifths a day. I never really intended to open or operate a halfway house for alcoholics. I just wanted to witness to a few about the peace and joy of recovery with a spiritual basis. However, God lured me into this situation and then like Noah when he went into the ark, God shut the door. I've not been able to leave since then, but as I do this work I have complete peace of mind. When I consider leaving it, I do not have peace of mind. So I continue amid advice from well-meaning folks who say, "You are crazy!" or "You'd better look out for yourself!"

I have never pretended that I have any gifts for healing or restoring alcoholics. I witness to my own experience and urge the alcoholic to get his own experience with God. Since I take no credit for those successes we have, I also take no responsibility for the failures. It is not my doing or my business. It is God's doing and God's business! God is our ever-present help in time of need. If an alcoholic wants that help, he will receive it. If he does not want it, he will never receive it.

Perhaps the greatest single message to an alcoholic anywhere is a small plaque found on the walls of most meeting rooms of Alcoholics Anonymous. It says simply: LET GO AND LET GOD!

If we have any secret formulas for recovery in our work, that is the only one I know about, and it is no secret! We too often stumble right over it because we look for complicated and time-related programs. Because we cannot presume to predict God's timetable, we have no time-related program. Indeed, we have no "program" at all. Each person is different, and each person must be dealt with as he can understand and learn. I have seen the "impossible" happen for a man who had nothing going for him. I have seen others with everything going who did not make it. I do not know why. I refuse to use all the tired old quotes so common with failure justification. This is all God's business. My business is just to witness to my own experience!

Isn't it terribly difficult to work with problem people who are alcoholics? It certainly is! You will flip your lid in a matter of weeks unless you have the extra help of the Lord. Unless you first realize just WHO gives the recovery, you are in for an awful time of disappointment and heartbreak. For this reason only those who have personal experience with alcoholism and a definite leading from the Lord should do it. Alcoholics are completely unpredictable and can be totally impossible. Without definite guidance from God, no "card-carrying" Christian (that's what I call a religionist) should ever try to deal with them.

Sincerity is not enough!

Your own love and compassion are not enough!

THE GRACE OF GOD IS THE ONLY HOPE! Let me say here, in love, that many well-meaning Christians have done much harm in a field they cannot understand. I have seen it.

New problems and new opportunities to see how God works have come with this experience. In supply and deliverance I am always keenly fascinated to be a part of it.

Let me say a few words about "deliverance" here. Any recovery from alcoholism which gives peace of mind and sobriety IS GOD'S DELIVERANCE! We tend to classify the Lord's miracles as being instant and someone else's work as being time-related. God did not instantly complete his creation. It took seven days with one day for rest! When God takes time, his time, for re-creating the mangled life of some wayward child, let us still give praise and credit where it is due, for God alone can do this. Nobody else can. Let's give thanks to God for those wonderful folks in our hospitals and detox-centers whom God uses to keep an alcoholic alive until he can make contact with God! They may not be overly spiritual. They may not have the twenty-third Psalm tattooed on their bodies, but God is using them in a very real way. After all, God once used a donkey to speak when it suited his purpose. I usually think of that when I am asked to speak somewhere! It is a most humbling realization for me!

There is a great personal joy when I see someone make a lasting recovery, get his family back together, and begin the adventure back into a world of reality. When I feel a tinge of personal credit coming on, I just allow myself a thought of how many others with the same opportunity did not make it. This is a great leveling exercise. I can take no credit for success! Neither do I have to accept feelings of guilt where there has been failure. I do not know all the answers. I have learned to be content with however and whenever God chooses to work. I am always aware of the one sheep for whom the Good Shepherd left ninety and nine in the fold and went on his search (see Matt. 18:12; Luke 15:4).

CHAPTER 9

SOME RAIN AND SOME RAINBOWS

For several years our halfway house was supported by our own efforts, mostly my own and the contributions of residents who got well and got jobs. My work was still in the entertainment business. This meant I was working with sick alcoholics in the daytime, then entertaining drunks in clubs at night. This gave me all day and half the night for a study of the effects of alcohol in the early and late stages. It was an education not often available to directors of halfway houses. In my twenty-five years in entertainment and my overlapping years working with alcoholics, I have seen about everything you can see of the use and abuse of alcohol. No study course could have given me this. I feel God never gives us a job to do without the knowledge to do that job. The Lord often uses strange ways to give us the knowledge and equipment we need.

This education was not confined to alcoholics. I have had a real and often testing series of lessons with "card-carrying" Christians. Fellow Christians seem to come in two groups (with respect to their thinking in regard to alcoholics).

There are those who wish to ignore the alcoholic, mainly because they just don't know how to cope with him. "He's a hopeless case," is their line of thinking. This is an easy and often used brush-off for people who are in the depths of despair and not easy to deal with. I still believe "With God, all things are possible," after all, I was "impossible."

I believe in miracles! I am one!

The other group is the "card-carrying, religionist" who oozes with sweet sayings about the greatness of our work. They assure us of their prayers for our efforts. They do this because it costs no money to pray, and they never invest their money in this area of the Lord's work! We found that Christians who will back you up with both money and prayer were too few to even form a group!

To me, this is sad, not because I am involved in alcoholic recovery, but because we seem to be bundled in little groups and congregations AND WE REFUSE TO BE INVOLVED IN ANY EFFORT WHICH DOES NOT BEAR THE STAMP OF OUR OWN LIMITED GROUP. I learned in my involvement with the church that I can belong to one congregation and visit many others. It is rather like a huge spiritual buffet, and we may as well sample all of it. I recall that I once mentioned my love for a well-known choir to a Christian friend. I was told, "Oh, but they are not Spirit-filled!"

I said, "Really! I was so busy enjoying the Lord blessing me through them that I hadn't noticed!"

God is UNLIMITED! We need to follow suit! How dreary to get in one little huddle and never experience anything outside our own little clan. God has all kinds of goodies and blessings, and I'll never know it unless I move around the buffet table of the Lord!

My education to Christian giving outside of a limited group was a shock. I knew my early traditional fundamentalist church did not even look outside its doors, but that was forty years ago! Surely the social revolution and the message of love has reached modern Christians. *MAY I REPORT THAT IN MANY CASES IT HAS NOT!* This does not mean God has not provided for our work in some amazing ways, but fellow Christians have never rushed forward with money for food or housing for alcoholics who are not well enough to provide for themselves as yet.

Did you know that the awful rumors of excess money, government grants, and money-making rackets usually do not come from bartenders or prostitutes?

They come from the gossip of fellow believers! This was another part of my difficult education.

I have always been amazed at the room for gossip in our fellowship of Christians. If my life is so crammed full with my relationship to the Lord in daily communion, I have no time left to talk about anyone! ONLY THOSE WHO HAVE ABSOLUTELY NOTHING GOING IN THEIR OWN LIVES AND EXPERIENCE HAVE TIME TO TALK ABOUT YOURS. Busy people are happy people. Busy people simply don't have time to gossip or listen to gossip. Rumors flew, but the Lord kept me too busy to hear them. My feeling was one of sadness that someone had such an empty life he had time for only idle talk.

Many of the people who came to us for help did not make it. They tried and failed and went on their way. Others made glowing recoveries and are still going.

God has never, in his wisdom, allowed me to see the whole scope of the outreach of our work, probably to protect my pride. But he has also never allowed me to see some of the failures in order to protect me from disappointment.

Our work is not limited to dealing with newcomers. Many times it is the man with several years sobriety who needs help. I remember one time a man came to the house for help who had recovered from active alcoholism a couple of years before. His problem was stress from job hunting. His mind was about to explode from pressure. We talked awhile about God being unlimited and that he supplied good jobs as well as alcoholic recovery. Then I had a strange leading to have our group lay hands on the man and pray for his stress and the return of peace of mind. We did just that! Can you imagine such a thing - a bunch of sober old drunks laying hands on another drunk to pray for his peace of mind? God must have laughed right out loud! But when he finished laughing, he gave the man such peace of mind he didn't even look like the same person. A short time later he had a job; a very good job!

I have learned to pray and allow a spirit of discernment to guide me in my work. It saves time and effort, and it places the time invested where it will do the most good. I have often spent an entire night with a newcomer who needed to talk it all out. I have often refused to spend five minutes with a man when my inner leading told me he was interested only in a place to sleep and something to eat and not in any spiritual help for recovery from his drinking problem. We feed anyone who is hungry. This is scriptural. We refer them to other houses when we feel they are not interested in spiritual recovery. If the Lord is going to direct this work, then I must follow his direction in all areas of it.

We have some rain with those who do not make a real recovery at the time of residence with us, but oh, the rainbows of those who do! Since God created both the rain and the rainbow, we must accept both. I am even now learning to stop asking "Why?" and rest in the assurance that God does indeed have "the whole world in his hands!"

CHAPTER 10
SOME OF THE ODDS AND ENDS

Mention sex in a group of Christians and half of them will faint while the other half stare at you as if they do not know the word! THIS IS NOT HONEST! NOT BEING HONEST, IT CAN'T BE CHRISTIAN! I am sick and tired of the puritanical idea that God created a body and then when he turned around and wasn't looking someone else put sex organs on it! When you deal with alcoholics, you must deal with the whole man and the whole problem honestly, clearly, and directly. When I tell my residents, "UNTIL YOU CAN PRAY ABOUT YOUR SEX LIFE YOU DON'T HAVE AN HONEST AND REALISTIC RELATIONSHIP WITH GOD," it is a direct statement of faith about a real problem of human beings. "God helps us from the waist up and we try to 'overcome' from the waist down" is as unrealistic as saying, "God created your hands but not your feet." We are God's children from the top of our heads to the tips of our toes. I am delighted to tell you that he can handle all problems in all areas of us! I know a lot of Christians who could use this idea of prayer for the whole man!

One man told me that he remembered our teaching about the whole man several years later and it worked. This was a man who had overcome a bad drug problem only to be overcome by the "lighter" problem with alcohol. Do you know what happened to him? He got squared away from all chemical addiction, and you would not even recognize him now. He founded a drug program for kids, is active in his church, and with his wife has reached over twelve hundred youngsters and their families. It never ceases to amaze me what our Lord can do with the completed whole person regardless of his or her past mistakes!

For alcoholics to just get sober and stay sober is a real miracle from our Lord, but for them to become involved and useful makes their lives and the lives of those whom they reach a much richer experience. It expands our outreach in so many ways and directions that we may never know about. As Gert Behanna says, "IT JUST SHOWS YOU WHAT ODDS AND ENDS OUR LORD CAN USE!" After all, he who has been forgiven much can love much. Those of us who have come back from near death are living and walking and talking examples of what a miracle is today! Jesus said, "He that believeth on me, the works that I do shall he do also; and greater works than these shall he do; because I go unto my Father." (John 14:12) It has been my privilege to see some of these greater things. I DON'T DO ANYTHING, BECAUSE I CAN'T DO ANYTHING. Often the greatest thing we can do is to live with some excitement and zest for what we have, and that we are over what we were.

Life is exciting and full! I am awake and aware of what is going on! I actually live life! I don't sleep through it in a daze of alcoholism.

I have problems, and I face them with prayer and hope. Most often I learn from each problem. CAN YOU IMAGINE A LIFE WITH ALL DAYS AND NO NIGHTS or all sunshine and no rain? All valleys and no hills would make pretty dull traveling. So when the Lord gives me some hill to climb and I get a little weary, I just remember that this exercise is good for my spiritual health. It develops spiritual muscles I may soon need in some new way. I am able to actually PRAISE THE LORD IN ALL THINGS!

This awareness of the value of problems was new to me. I had some idea that God took us under his wing never again to face difficulty. This would be like an earthly father who carried his child all his life and never allowed him to take a few falls learning to walk. The Lord holds my hand. I often need to sit at his knee and talk it all out, but he never seems to carry me. He does teach me to walk - upright and with balance!

CHAPTER II

TO BE IN THE WORLD, BUT NOT OF THE WORLD

"If ye were of the world, the world would love his own: but because ye are not of the world, but I have chosen you out of the world, therefore the world hateth you." (John 15:19)

"They are not of the world, even as I am not of the world." (John 17:16)

To be "in the world" but not "of the world" was a new lesson for me. I had been taught that we come apart and make ourselves separate from all that is worldly. The religionist's definition of what constituted worldliness was even more confusing. I always wondered how such complete separateness could possibly reach anyone new with the news of Jesus Christ.

When I discovered that there was a vast difference between mere religion and vibrant Christianity I learned that we need not only be *in* the world, but we are to be up to our ears *in* it if we are going to reach anyone with the Gospel. WE MUST BE WITH PEOPLE IF WE ARE GOING TO TALK TO THEM. Sending little notes to the outside world from the safe fold of some Sunday School room is just not effective. I found that our Lord, by his example and teaching, not only allowed us to be in the world, but instructed us to *go into the world* and tell everyone about his truth.

In my case, being *in* the world, but not *of* the world, meant being an entertainer in night clubs for seven more years after my conversion experience. What better place! What place can you find with more need? The openers were all set. People who had seen me perform before, so drunk that I leaned on my instrument as much as I played it, now wanted to know what had happened in my life! They were eager to know and I was eager to tell them! This is witnessing - simple and direct, telling what had happened in my life. I was under God's instructions to do so, and the Holy Spirit's ability to do so. Never did I feel led to beat anybody to death with a Bible. Never did I feel led to tell anyone they must have the same experience in their own lives. Sometimes we get overzealous and go off on a crusade of our own design. This is more harmful than no witness at all.

People are already beaten down with the cares of the world. If I, in my own enthusiasm, beat them down with orders of what they must do, I fail completely. I may use the same enthusiasm to lift up Christ and my experience with him. Then it is my job to GET OUT OF THE WAY AND LET JESUS CHRIST DRAW THEM TO HIMSELF, in his time and in his way.

I never once had to make an opening for a witness for Jesus Christ and my own experience. The questions were always there. They have always been there with the alcoholics I work with. I never had to say, "Look what happened to me!" I just lived my life as I was led to live it, and they asked, "What happened to you?"

If you are witnessing for the Lord, YOU NEVER NEED MAKE AN OPPORTUNITY. Just be ready to witness and THE SAME LORD WHO GIVES THE WITNESS WILL GIVE THE OPPORTUNITY! To do otherwise is sometimes running ahead of God's plan, and we never want to be way off in front of God. We need to be right there at the right time and right alongside the Lord. If we have a witness which falls on deaf ears, they may be deaf to us because the Lord, by the power of the Holy Spirit, has not opened them up yet. We must be alert to God's timing.

We may be out of time with the Lord. My experience in music has taught me the value of timing. Music which is out of time is a mess, and it is never beautiful. So it is with God's timing. We are never out of line when we align ourselves with the timing of the Lord. He is never wrong, no matter how far-out it may seem. Witnessing in a nightclub - where you are paid an excellent wage to entertain people so they will spend more money at the bar - is a pretty farout place and way to witness to the changing power of Jesus Christ. Yet, I was never out of line and never once did any manager speak to me about hurting business with my ideas which were contrary to a need for a drink in the first place. Let me assure you that a club owner does not want any employee to do or say anything which might hurt the bar business. LET ME ALSO ASSURE YOU THAT BY NATURE I AM NOT THAT BOLD. I am a total and complete conformist and want to fit in wherever I am. Yet, no matter how shy you are and how sedate and quiet, when the joy of the Lord bubbles up from deep inside you, YOU WILL TALK ABOUT IT!

I never was, and never could be, a Sunday Christian. Either Christianity is a bubbling and exciting experience seven days a week, anywhere and everywhere I go, or I have some kind of religion which I can use for an hour and then put it in a nice velvet case until next Sunday. Christianity is not a place to go on Sunday, or a bit of dogma to recite. It is a way of living, and I live all week. Indeed, my Christianity has never served me as well on a nice Sunday as it does on a hot Tuesday afternoon with a new problem drunk on my hands. Your work may not be with drunks, but whatever you do, your Christianity should also work for you on a hot Tuesday afternoon!

Christianity changes us. It certainly changed me. I was a chic and sophisticated sort of person, terribly frightened of not being accepted and doing the correct thing at the correct time. I was so socially conscious that I often wonder if I wanted to go to heaven after death or just go to Neiman-Marcus and be very stylish throughout eternity! But an experience with Jesus Christ can make a blabbermouth out of the most shy person you ever saw. At the right time and in the right place you can't shut me up. When the Lord does not lead me to speak out, I am still very quiet. But when it suits his purpose, the

Lord will use a donkey to speak, or he may use a quiet and shy musician who could not sell a thing otherwise.

CHAPTER 12
THE GIFT OF EXPERIENCE

Did you ever wonder, "Why me, Lord?" when some difficult experience comes your way? I have many times. I had the mistaken idea that the Lord gave perfect peace because we had perfect lives. With all that smooth sailing, who could be troubled? However, I learned that God's perfect peace lasts right in the middle of a problem, and it is not the absence of difficult times that gives us peace. But the experience gained with heartbreaking problems gives insight and feeling in later dealing with others who have a similar problem.

My deliverance from alcoholism was simply a miracle of survival. BUT WHO WANTS JUST SURVIVAL? My personal and daily relationship with Jesus Christ has made that survival a real adventure! I never know what will happen next! Each day is a whole world in itself, and I am constantly amazed at the variations of the Lord's goodness.

I have known rejection to the point of heartbreak. So when I deal with someone who has bitterness because of rejection, there is that understanding bought with experience. I have known loneliness so real you could almost speak to it as a gloomy entity. So when I deal with the loneliness of others I understand their feelings. I SPEAK THEIR LANGUAGE. I have known heartbreak and disappointment so great that it wilted my spirit for a time. When I deal with the heartbreak of others I am keenly aware of their hurt.

Nothing can come my way as a child of God without his permission. God has a purpose for all that he does or allows. The purpose of experience is too obvious in my life. I HAVE NEVER HAD A DIFFICULT EXPERIENCE WHICH I HAVE NOT DEALT WITH LATER IN THE LIVES OF OTHERS. Without my own scars I would simply be talking in vague terms about something I really did not understand. I can't get real feeling from reading about some tragedy in a condensed version of Reader's Digest! Having lived it, I can speak from the depths of my heart in Christian love and understanding. I can say I know because I do know the hurt. I can say, "This, too, will pass," because in my own life it has all passed, and I am here and alive and happy to tell about it.

I have learned to trust God's purpose in all things - good and bad. If my house burns down, I must simply know that God plans to give me a better one, or that I will soon deal with someone who has known great material loss and I will need that experience to witness effectively. For all the other difficult things which happen in my life, I always find an opportunity to witness and deal effectively with a person who has the same problem.

God's schooling is not easy, but he never gives any trial or hard experience for which grace to stand and overcome is not in abundant supply!

Out of all of this we can grow and learn and become equipped to witness with understanding and feeling. This has been consistently true in my life. I believe it is all a part of our Lord's magnificent plan for our lives.

No hurt lasts longer than it takes to bring it to God and ask for a removal of the pain, *not the removal of the problem, but its effect on me.* IT IS NOT WHAT HAPPENS TO ME, BUT MY REACTION THAT COUNTS. I have learned to ask God to change me and my reaction, never to remove the problem or the concern for someone else who may be a part of that problem. If I have a return of perfect peace, then it really doesn't matter what is happening around me. Jesus once spoke to a storm and it ceased. He can and does speak to the storm within our minds and souls, and they also obey his word!

We develop spiritual muscles with trials. No fighter ever read a book on fighting and then went into a ring to try his luck with personal experience. No, he usually has a great training time and many actual practice fights to get in shape for the big ones. So it is with us. When we have a spiritual exercise session and some problems which upset us, we develop spiritual muscles and tone up for more strength which will be needed later. We learn by doing and being a part of life, all of life. The difficult trials often allow us to shed some of our false values and get back on the right theme with more realistic Christian values.

CHAPTER 13
RELIGION IS OFTEN BIG BUSINESS, CHRISTIANITY IS NOT

Too often when I discuss the various problems of my work with clergymen I am amazed at their attitudes. I think the next time a minister says to me, "But on the practical side ...," I shall break down and cry! I am sorry, gentlemen, but I believe that CHRISTIANITY IS THE PRACTICAL SIDE!

The simplicity of the teachings of Jesus Christ do not always follow the best of hard-core business principles. After all, if you continue to "turn the other cheek," YOU CAN LOSE A LOT OF CHEEKS THAT WAY. It is not a sound investment of cheeks by strict practicality. Certainly we must have some order and some organization. I cannot work without it any more than you can. However, we can get so chartered and so organized that WE ORGANIZE THE QUIET AND SOFT LEADING OF THE HOLY SPIRIT RIGHT OUT OF OUR EFFORTS. We find ourselves all organized with no results. The Holy Spirit organizes little and big businesses, but God always provides when we trust him.

I am no fool. I grew up "backstage" at the church, and there's not a revival trick of the 1930s I don't know and couldn't use. I am well aware that there is a fast and plenty buck in religion. "THERE'S GOLD IN THEM THERE SCRIPTURAL HILLS" if that is what I want. However, having already found that gold brings no peace, it is easier for me to skip the tricks and gimmicks and stick to simple Christianity. I spent twenty-five years in show business. I can spot a performance five miles away in a fog! All I need to do is follow the simple and quiet direction of our Lord. No blue follow spots. No press releases, and no percentage guarantees except the ones made by Jesus Christ to supply all my needs. HE HAS NEVER FAILED YET, and I have no reason to believe he will ever fail me. It would take another complete book just to cover the various ways and means God has used to provide for my work without great effort or concern on my part. We are told not to be concerned with material things, and I am not.

It's not the size of the budget you need to meet, but the shape of your heart that marks the difference between religion and Christianity.

CHAPTER 14

REQUESTS AND DELIVERIES

Southern summers are hot and humid and we had a houseful of new residents in the middle of a hot gulf coast summer. It was at this time our central air-conditioning system broke, and it is not always possible to get building owners to quickly invest in necessary repairs when they are expensive. This was our experience and I did what I always do when I am faced with an "impossible" situation; I went into my room and began one of my short and direct talks with God on our need for cool air.

You know what happened? The very next incoming alcoholic resident was an air-conditioning specialist and he got our big house cooled off in short order. It was a special kind of cool, knowing it was an answer to prayer. And the incoming resident found the joy of being needed by us at the same time he needed our message of recovery for his problem. This all happened in a matter of a few days.

A short time later we were given some very good chests of drawers and a large desk, a great amount of new carpeting, and a wonderful new divan for the lounge. These were gifts from interested Christian friends and we were delighted. Only one problem. We did not have a truck to pick up all the things and get them from the homes of the donors to our house. Well, what do you do with a problem? You take it to the Lord. It is just not reasonable that God would inspire people to give us things we needed and not also supply a means to get them transported. So back I went to my room and prayed, "Lord, we need to get these things over to the house and you will have to handle it for us." Know what happened? That's right! The very next resident came to us driving a pickup truck. He needed us and we needed him. So we took off in his truck and got every single item that had been given to us. Coincidence? I do not believe so. We rarely get a new resident with a car. Almost never one with a truck. Thank you Lord!

Sometime later we found a leak in the roof of a huge storage closet where we keep donated clothes for residents who come to us with nothing but the clothes on their bodies. We had to take the clothes out and store them on a bed which we needed for new people. Again, our building owner was slow to invest in such costly repairs.

Back I went to my room and my REAL source of supply for *all* needs. I said, "Lord, we need that roof fixed soon and you know how to get it done." I got a call that night from a man who needed residence and our message of recovery and deliverance. By "coincidence" he just happened to be a roofer by trade. I said,'-'Boy, do we ever need you." And we did! He got our roof fixed and the room is as dry as a church service where the Spirit of the Lord is absent.

We thanked the Lord for the new roof and zoomed along with our work with clothes for the needy, food for the hungry, and a new testimony of hope for those addicted to alcohol.

Once we desperately needed a cook. I was in the kitchen between the exit of our last cook and the finding of a new one. I was up to my ears in cabbage, meat and potatoes. I was complaining about it because it was just too much work with all the other things I had to do. I suddenly realized that I was spending much energy on complaining when I could invest that same energy and action in prayer for help. You know, I have come to realize that God will often let us work too hard and wear ourselves down when we insist on doing it and forget to literally take our burden and our need to him in prayer.

I redirected my energy and began to ask the Lord to bring a cook to us - one that needed us as badly as we needed him. Need I tell you that in short order we had a new man who needed us, one who could cook like a dream, cut food costs like a miracle, and loved our work!

You see, we can complain to God about the stress and the strain of our work, or we can request help to meet the needs of our work and we can get that help. If I get busy with a "poor me" performance and forget the real source of all help, I am in trouble. If I "Praise God in all things" and request help, I always get the needed help. Without exception, if I get bogged down in too much work or too many needs, it is simply my own fault for not looking to God for *every* need and expecting his supply to come.

Automobile repair is expensive for all of us. It can be a devastating problem when you operate on a low budget. This has not been a single experience in our work. Several times our cars have needed repair and I have simply asked God to handle it for me. Always a man comes to us quickly who can do whatever repair we need at the small cost of parts.

I was asked to do a TV program and speak about deliverance from alcoholism, my own, and those we deal with. I thought "What shall I wear?" Most of my clothes are old and not too good for such an appearance. Know what happened? A friend insisted that I accept a new outfit I had admired. It was a fire-engine-red outfit which perfectly suited my need. This updated my dress appearance. May I say my faith was updated too! Today's needs are taken to our Lord in prayer and supplied!

Last year we began a garden project to add fresh food to our town house operation. We had the seeds and the soil and the interest, but nobody had any real knowledge of growing things. So I sent up my request, "Lord, you gave us the seeds and the equipment and we need someone who knows how to use them properly." Our very next resident came to us with a farm background you wouldn't believe! The next year it happened again. Coincidence? I don't believe so. We get many people who love plants but know little about them. It takes a very special person to grow all the things we produce. We always get that special person at the right time!

Sound like a dreamworld? If you will read Genesis you will remember that God created this world as a dreamworld. It was the fall of Adam and Eve which messed it up. Let me quickly state that Jesus Christ restored our status with God and we can again have dominion over our needs and problems if we ask in his name, believing.

Impossible things are happening every day! Each time I run into a brick wall of trouble I try to stop and remember the word of our Lord that "With men this *is* impossible; but with God *all* things are possible!" (Matt. 19:26) This is an exciting, adventurous, wonderful way to live and entirely necessary for me in this work! I often remember Jesus' words to the followers of his time, "O ye of little faith." (Matt. 16:8) I wonder if things are not about the same two thousand years later. If there is lack, it is not God's fault. It is mine.

In our needs I often wonder if we are not driving wagons when we could and should be driving Cadillacs! I wonder if sometimes we don't wallow in totally unnecessary want when it is our Father's good pleasure to supply loads of good things to his children. I have several times prayed a simple prayer, "Lord, please deliver me of a poverty complex and get my aim a little higher!"

Certainly reality Christianity will not allow us to be hung up on possessions. But there are times when I hear loud and clear, YE HAVE NOT BECAUSE YE ASK NOT! I am ashamed of myself. A professing Christian and a CHILD OF THE KING who carries on like a pauper!

I have mentioned several little daily miracles I remember, but I have left out hundreds more for lack of time and space to witness to each incident.

Sometimes my eyes fill with tears at the wonder of it all! God has declared himself to be willing, able, and even anxious to give us the desires of our hearts. Now if I can just get my aim a little higher and my belief in action, who knows what great and good things our Lord has in store for me here and now today!

When I read again about the rich young ruler who was told to sell all his goods and give to the poor, I was actually happy that my hang-up with treasures and goodies had come to an end. The poor man simply could not let go of his treasures, because he had a lot. This story spoke to me plainly in terms I could understand that I need always KEEP MY CHRISTIANITY SIMPLE AND MY EARTHLY HOLDINGS THE SAME WAY. If possessions gave peace, then millionaires would all be happy and poor people would all be miserable. This is most often not true at all. From my years of travel in the entertainment business I recall that the most unhappy people I met were the ones with great wealth.

There is nothing wrong with great wealth. I know a few very wealthy people who have peace, but their peace comes from our Lord, not from their wealth. However, it is a dangerous place to be! There comes the time when God may desire to separate us from our holdings for his own reasons. Then we may not find it so easy to retain peace, but when we do, he bountifully blesses.

Suppose when we get to heaven we find that we have an allowance to spend for all eternity based solely on what we gave away on earth for the causes of our Lord. Can you imagine trying to make it all through eternity ON SUNDAY SCHOOL PENNIES! Or some meager sum we gave a church! I often wonder if God doesn't have some very real accounting plan like that for our laying up treasures in heaven when our savings will be free from earthly losses.

Over the big hurdles of loving my fellowman as I love myself, and the big one of possessions, I was now ready for other lessons, new classes, and more growing.

Would you believe that all this time I was still an entertainer in nightclubs? For seven years the Lord let me stay in the middle of a variety of "dens of sin." What better place to give a witness to the deliverance of Jesus Christ from alcoholism? This was the "highways and byways," that the Bible talks about, and I was planting seeds like no entertainer had ever done before - never pushy and never preachy - just answering questions. After all, a musician who does not drink has a perfect opening. We had hundreds of quick question-and-answer periods in those years. I may never know the end results of those seeds, but I did know the joy of planting! And if I lift up Christ, then he said he would do the drawing of men to himself (see John 12:32). Producing a finished product is not my business. It is the business of Almighty God.

The teachings of Jesus on love and possessions were not just some pretty writing I could read like a Shakespearean sonnet! They were actual rules to live by. Since I had this understanding, it had to be followed by action. Religionists might skip them. I, as a seeking Christian, could not. This was no great problem because I had already tried the barren desert of worldly possessions and was certainly ready for some of our Lord's green pastures and still waters.

I shall forever be grateful for the simplicity of learning that love for my fellowman and the right understanding about possessions are two of the most difficult lessons to learn, and are the gateway to a whole new world. I'm no saint. I'm about as average as they come. I didn't really love anybody. I talked about love for others, but it was all talk, and I didn't have any real love. I was just as hung up on possessions, security, money, and the whole bit as the next guy.

You can't have the security myth of the American way of life drummed into your mind for thirty years without it becoming a part of your thinking. IT IS THE PERSONAL CONTACT WITH JESUS CHRIST WHICH CHANGES ALL THAT! I didn't "give up" a thing. It simply all fell away and I found a whole new set of values. Old things did pass away and I was a new creature with new goals (see II Cor. 5:17). I have had people say, "How can you live like this?" And I really don't know how, except that the old ideas are gone and I now have more peace and security than I ever had with all the things our society calls security.

Won't I grow old without all the preparations and provisions I may need to care for me in my old age? Why should I? God has provided in some unusual ways for my care and my work. There is no reason to think he will end his provision at age 65 or 70. We have an excellent working arrangement. He provides the means, and I provide the work. *He has never failed in his provision.*

Once in an old house where we had recovering alcoholics, we were about to run out of funds to keep open. I called my booking agent to book another contract in a club to keep us going, but no contract was to be had in the city. The closest was eighty miles away. I could not play eighty miles away and run the house and work with the men who were new to alcoholic recovery.

I prayed a short prayer which went something like this, "Okay, God, it's really your house and if you want to close it, it's fine with me. If you want to keep it open, then you had better do something fast." Do you know what happened? We got a check in the mail for one thousand dollars from an unsolicited source, a man who is very conservative and never gave us a dime before, nor has he since. When God decides to use you, rest assured he will be your source.

Another time in a similar situation the telephone rang and a lady gave us five thousand dollars' worth of Exxon stock! I am always grateful to God for these miracles of provision, but I have also come to expect them. It is part of our simple working agreement!

Those Jesus chose to follow him were asked to leave whatever they were doing and simply follow him. They did just that! They were all cared for in every way! Following this example I feel I cannot do otherwise. No part-time arrangement and no half commitments. This is for me! Maybe it is not for everyone, but my understanding requires this action. As a religionist I could read ABOUT such action. As a Christian I MUST BECOME INVOLVED WITH HIM PERSONALLY. When I do, my entire world turns upside down and I am never the same person again!

CHAPTER 15
SILK PURSES MADE FROM SOW'S EARS!

After seeing some of the lost people we deal with in alcoholic recovery, many Christians have said to me, "Well, you can't make a silk purse out of a sow's ear." Well, I can't even make a silk purse out of silk! But let me tell you without apology that our Lord Jesus Christ can and does make silk purses out of most anything available and willing to be re-created!

I BELIEVE IN MIRACLES! I AM ONE!

I have seen so many come from nothing into THE SOMETHING OF GOD!

"How can you stand to be around such trash?" people say to me.

"What better place to serve?" is my response to them.

I am amazed at the number of "card-carrying" Christians who seem to think Jesus belonged to a Bethlehem Country Club and was always in the company of nice, chic, and acceptable folks. The scriptures state otherwise. Jesus was often criticized for his association with sinners and tax collectors and wayward folks. His answer was classic: "Sick people need the doctor, not healthy ones! I haven't come to tell good people to repent, but the bad ones." (Mark 2:17 TLB)

Those who came to Christ were in physical and mental and spiritual need. MARY MAGDALENE WAS NOT EXACTLY A MEMBER OF THE JUNIOR LEAGUE WHEN SHE CAME TO JESUS! But how the Lord changed her life and her class! This certainly was an example of re-creation by our Lord. Let me assure you that the re-creation goes on in this day in exactly the same way.

I know my own experience was much the same. I had a definite class consciousness, and I am still aware of it, but I do believe in the scriptural fact of equal opportunity for all of God's children. A long time ago when I first began working with problem people, I wondered what people would think about my association with this "class" of folks. It was some time later that I learned most people really don't think with any degree of regularity. They could care less what I do if they are not personally involved. I find this true in most religious circles where people tell me they "have no calling" to be involved out of their immediate circle. They stay away, and they keep their checkbooks with them. This leaves those of us who are involved free to work without the distractions or support of such people. Their ideas are their own, AND THEIR ANSWERS TO GOD MUST BE THEIR OWN!

I have been accused of "casting my pearls before swine" (see Matt. 7:6) in passing on the Good News of deliverance through Jesus Christ to "tacky old alcoholics." Really now, that's a bit much! True, some of these people turn and walk away from any deliverance and recovery. But so did the rich young ruler who came to Jesus asking how to be saved. It is not my business to chain people to a chair and beat them into submission. I present the news of what I have experienced and seen, and I offer each of them an opportunity to make initial contact with GOD, AS HE UNDERSTANDS HIM - as that individual understands God - and go from there. I lift up Jesus Christ and then try to get out of the way so Jesus can do the drawing. If this is "casting my pearls before swine," then I need a lot more pearls, and I hope the Lord will continue to send me all the "swine" he has out there!

CHAPTER 16

THE GREATEST OF THESE IS LOVE!

Relating to St. Paul as a person has always been kind of hard for me. I know you're not supposed to admit a thing like this, but if I am to be honest, then I must admit it. Paul was always like a District Superintendent, and I never did care for District Superintendents! They were always telling people what to do and where they were wrong. I could never imagine wanting to get close to Paul and be with him. He would make me very nervous and uncomfortable. Other apostles and writers I love and could get close to, but Paul as a person always left me quite cold. I know one day I shall meet Paul, and then I'll feel his inner warmth.

But from Paul we get some of the most glorious writing known to man. That just shows you what God can do! Take a cantankerous old District Superintendent and through him produce life-giving words! The greatest single writing on LOVE ever given to man is written by Paul in I Corinthians, chapter thirteen. Here Paul gives the value of love and the utter loss we face without it. He makes it quite plain that no matter how many other goodies and gifts we may have, if we don't have love we don't really have a thing! I found this true in my own experience. There is absolutely nothing I could add to the thirteenth chapter of I Corinthians, but I can make a suggestion. It is a short and direct chapter. READ IT EVERY MORNING FOR THIRTY DAYS AND SEE WHAT HAPPENS IN YOUR LIFE. Something supernatural happens when I read and re-read this amazing definition of love and its importance and application to my life.

If you are planning to "walk on water," or polish up your halo and go some place really nice, by all means take a thirty-day break and read this love chapter every day before you take off. You'll be delighted at how this truth will become a part of your thinking, and amazed at how it puts everything back into proper perspective!

CHAPTER 17
GODLY INDIVIDUALITY

Jesus said, "And other sheep I have, which are not of this fold; them also I must bring." (John 10:16a) HOW COULD HE! Other sheep who may not be a member of my congregation? Oh GOD, THEY MIGHT NOT EVEN BE CHARISMATIC! OH GOD, THEY MIGHT *EVEN* BE CHARISMATIC! And to think that he said he had to bring them too! Maybe they won't fit in. Maybe I won't like them. What we need is more restrictions on who gets in and who does not! When will we ever learn that God created INDIVIDUALS, and people got together and created GROUPS.

God does not deal with each of us in the same way. I do not know of any two Christians who have had the exact same experiences at the same time. Growth patterns are vastly different. THIS IS GOD-GIVEN INDIVIDUALITY. It is a part of the glorious variations of all creation. To try to make duplicates or insist on copies is a mistake - man's mistake! GOD DOES NOT DEAL IN CHEAP CARBON COPIES. HE DEALS IN WONDERFUL ORIGINALS.

I have my experiences and my work. You have yours. We may share, but we can never duplicate. When we try to copy each other, we usually end up with a spiritual mess.

It took me a long, long time to adjust to the "other sheep" of Jesus' fold. I think I have met some of them. If he said he must bring them also, then it is quite all right with me. How and when he brings them is not under my direction. If I presume to get into this business, I am presuming on Almighty God, and that is too much presuming!

Did you know that if I experience the real love of Christ in my heart, then godly individuality is not a hard thing to accept at all? If Jesus wants to bring them, can't I agree? If Jesus forgives them, can't I forgive them, too? If Jesus looks on the inside and accepts them, then it does not really matter whether I accept them or not, except that my failure to accept them MAY MAR MY OWN RELATIONSHIP WITH OUR LORD.

Remember when some of the followers of Jesus came up to him and told him that they saw a man using Jesus' name to cast out demons? They said, "We told him not to. After all, he isn't in our group." (Luke 9:49 TLB) Remember Jesus' answer? Look it up in the "Book." Jesus said, "You shouldn't have done that! For anyone who is not against you is for you." (vs. 50) The "Book" is the last place most of us go to find the answers. IT SHOULD BE THE FIRST PLACE! Things have not changed in two thousand years. We still seem to think the wonders of Almighty God are franchised like Colonel Sander's Fried Chicken. If we have a franchise, we may then share the Good News. Can't we then loosen up a bit and claim our own individuality in the Lord, allowing others to do the same thing? Can't we love each other that much?

I have been a visitor in churches where great gifts were in evidence. In the midst of all this I found a "closed shop" attitude which let me know in no uncertain terms that I must be "another sheep from another fold." This, I learned, was done to protect themselves from "evil outside influences." Sorry brothers, but I am under the definite impression that GOD IS ALL POWERFUL AND HE CAN AND HE WILL PROTECT WHAT IS HIS FROM ANY AND ALL OUTSIDE FORCES. Jesus said the gates of hell would not prevail against his church. I believe it. If we are full of fear of outside evils, then we need more perfect love, because "PERFECT LOVE CASTETH OUT FEAR!" (I John 4:18)

God has all kinds of children. Since they are his children, they must be my brothers and sisters. Whatever their stages of growth and grace, I must love them and accept them as they are. Can you imagine a world where all trees and plants looked exactly alike? What a bore! But God created infinite variety in all of nature. YOU'LL FIND THE SAME VARIETY IN HIS CHILDREN!

CHAPTER 18

ON JOINING A CHURCH

It took me seven years after my recovery from alcoholism and my experiences with the Lord to join a church. I had no plan to join at that time. Strange are the ways and leadings of our Lord. I wasn't really anti-church, because I went to weddings and funerals when these came about. However, my own early experience with a fundamentalist church had been so very dismal and I had such a real thing going with Jesus Christ, that I was actually fearful that association with a church might diminish this reality. It was as if I had a lovely park all to myself and I was afraid someone might put a freeway through it in the name of "progress."

How did the Lord lead me, frightened to death, into a church membership? In the strangest way you can imagine! Here again is the real adventure of Christianity. THERE IS NEVER A DULL ACT WHEN THE LORD IS DIRECTING OUR SHOW!

I had offered my services to play music for a young people's recovery group when their second anniversary came up. The party was to be held on the lovely patio of a church. I figured if I didn't have to go inside and become a part of something, this would be a safe situation.

The party was delightful, and the music was fun. Then I learned that the minister of the church was present! He came walking across the patio looking exactly as if he had chewed up a neon sign and was aglow with the love and feeling that I had never seen in a minister before. He was smiling and hugging people, and it was real! This was no phony smile of "How nice to see you. Did you pay your pledge?" which I had come to expect from religionists. Then he came my way and spoke. I remembered the scripture which said, "Behold, how he loved him!" (John II:36) I was instantly and permanently hooked on the love of Jesus Christ which this man showed. I am well aware of all the professional charm one can use. I used it myself for many years in the entertainment business. This was different. It was simply and powerfully THE LOVE OF JESUS GOING THROUGH A CHRISTIAN AND REACHING OUT TO OTHERS.

I have never known this minister to walk on water, heal anyone, or multiply food supplies! But, I have also NEVER SEEN SUCH CHRISTIAN LOVE RADIATE FROM ANY OTHER BELIEVER IN QUITE THE SAME WAY. Every time I see him I am reminded of Paul's writing on love: "Though I speak with the tongues of men and of angels, and have not charity (love) . . .it profiteth me nothing." (I Cor. 13)

I knew a recovered drunk who joined this church; his witness was simple and direct on church membership. He said, "The Lord has done so much for me it seems little to return by a public confession of faith by spending time in church each week." He also gave me a small book on the history and belief of the church. The Lord cinched his direction by putting a hunger in my heart to be a part of something so lovely and real - I, who had been frightened to death of church membership, was hungry to be in it up to my earlobes! That's what God's love can do when it radiates through one of his active believers!

I took instruction in the faith. Me? Take instruction when I likely knew more Bible than those teaching the class? Yes, sir! I had to come "as a little child" free of my own knowledge and eager to learn again the simplicity of Christianity. I LOVED EVERY MINUTE OF IT! This again is what the Lord can do when we are willing to shut up and open up to teaching. I have found new meaning and new fellowship which I never had before in church membership. I love the feeling of being part of a family of Christians and A REAL AND VITAL PART OF THE BODY OF CHRIST. It gives a dimension I never knew as a private Christian without the family ties of a church. A few years ago, if someone had told me I would feel this way, I would have laughed right out loud.

Because the fundamentalist church I had known offered the communion with a strict and constant chant about being "worthy," I never took communion until I was way past forty! This was a part of my early negative training, and I never learned where one went to take lessons and get "worthy." With my new church family and re-reading scripture, I learned that we come to the Lord by his mercy and never by our own merit or worthiness.

I have worshiped with communion for several years now. If, for some reason, I miss the service, I am keenly aware of this all the following week. The adventure of Christianity is a constant delight, and communion is a necessary part of that adventure. Church membership came by direction, not by my own searching, and with it a whole new growth in Christianity. WITHIN THIS BROAD FRAMEWORK OF THE FAMILY OF CHRISTIANS I AM ALLOWED TO HAVE WHATEVER EXPERIENCES AND BLESSINGS OUR LORD GIVES ME. We are not bound by any great dogmas or restrictions.

Recently a well-meaning lady learned I was an Episcopalian and she said to me, "How do you stand it?" I knew her intentions were good even though her understanding was lacking, so I answered, "Stand it? I love it! This is where the Lord placed me, and until he moves me I am having a ball!" So, each Sunday and often during the week, you'll find me going to my church to publicly declare that I am a follower of Jesus Christ and to worship and seek strength for all the week.

CHAPTER 19

ENCOUNTER WITH AN OLD FRIEND

It pains me to share this experience with you, but I must, for I feel there is something to be learned from it.

A former drinking companion and friend of twenty-five years became a Christian and has been used by the Lord in my life several times. We shared various experiences over the new years of Christianity, and we both were blessed by this sharing. This was a sharing in love and fellowship.

Recently I received a series of letters from this Christian friend which were amazing. He had gotten on some sort of new kick of lashing out at those who did not totally agree with his latest learning and experience. The sharing letters had about as much love as the Spanish Inquisition or The Crusades! According to his theological concept, I was "in the flesh and not in the Spirit" and a whole mess of other instructional tidbits. My understanding of the Gospels was not led of the Holy Spirit but of some evil force which was confusing me. On and on this good friend went in a whiplash kind of instruction which had me dizzy from the scorn of it. The lack of love was so evident that I had no question in my mind but that Satan was again working from the INSIDE to bring hurt and disillusionment to believers.

SATAN NEVER WORKS SO FIERCELY OUTSIDE AS HE DOES FROM THE INSIDE IN CHRISTIAN CIRCLES. Because I am aware of this, I wrote my old friend and said, "Unless we can share in Christian love we should not share at all." I meant it! What began years ago as a wonderful sharing of various truths and experiences has bogged down into an ugly and argumentive exchange which is not worthy of the name "Christian." I want no part of it. From this painful experience I learned again that God looks on the inside while man looks on the outside. We need to be very careful when we set out to correct others in their understanding and experience. The Bible says, "Try the spirits," and we need to be absolutely sure JUST WHICH SPIRIT IS LEADING US INTO AN ACT OF STRONG CORRECTION. If it can be done with complete and unquestionable love, then we may be on the right track. If the action is ugly and lacking in love, then we better take another look at our guidance and seek out a Spirit of Truth.

I am not deaf to correction. Some of the greatest letters to come my way have been those from respected Christians in which they gently and firmly gave me correction. I am thankful for all of it. I learn from it and it has all been done in such love you could feel it in each page.

The saddest thing of all is that this old friend, who had been such a source of inspiration and blessing to me, seems now forever lost to me as a sharing fellow believer. Praise God, Jesus never has us with only one support for a foundation. OLD FRIENDS COME AND GO, BUT JESUS CHRIST IS THE SAME YESTERDAY, TODAY, AND FOREVER!

Let's be very careful that what we do and say is done ALWAYS IN CHRISTIAN LOVE! It's so easy to rub holes in weak Christian material when we apply "religious" friction where we should anoint with smooth love.

CHAPTER 20
MEETING EXCITED CHRISTIANS!

I have met very few truly excited Christians in my time. Most of them seem to be just barely making it as if God had some sort of brinksmanship act going which constantly grabbed them just as they were going over the cliff! Others are so quietly Christian you'd hardly notice except when they get in trouble and begin to yell for God to help! A few old recovered drunks I know have come from so far down that they have some excitement about where the Lord has brought them and are eager to talk about it. But for the most part, I was excited, but I could find few people who shared my excitement. Then someone handed me a book by Charles and Frances Hunter with some bland statement, "You might enjoy getting to know these folks since they live in your city."

I read the book, then went right out and bought all the rest of the books by Charles and Frances Hunter. HERE WERE PEOPLE WHO HAD SUCH EXCITEMENT ABOUT CHRISTIANITY IT SHOUTED FROM EVERY PAGE! As I finished each book I passed it on to an alcoholic resident in the house - small books, easy to read, and not some staggering work full of theory. Can you imagine a houseful of old drunks, each with a spiritual book, waiting for the exchange of another? This was another working of our Lord - EXCITING CHRISTIANITY IN A BOOK. In cases where I had failed to communicate the adventure of Christianity to residents, THE BOOKS WERE DOING IT! Then came the day we had finished all the books, and I asked if the residents would like to attend a meeting where the Hunters were witnessing. To be sure that they understood this was not exactly "high church" Episcopalian, I explained that the Hunters were "charismatic" and that unusual things happened in their meetings. THEY STILL WANTED TO GO!

In the meantime, I had exchanged letters with the Hunters, and they invited me to bring all the alcoholics we had, sober or drunk. We don't have any drunk alcoholics, only those who have been "detoxified" and are eager to learn to stay sober. So, off we went, a whole carload of freshly sober alcoholics, GOING TO THEIR VERY FIRST CHARISMATIC MEETING! We sat way back in the church, a whole row of us. We watched and waited to see what would happen. I have never in my life been so amused. There was a long line of alcoholics who had all been in various jails and institutions, mental hospitals and drying-out clinics, all sitting perfectly straight AND FRIGHTENED TO DEATH THAT SOMEONE MIGHT SEE THEM AND THINK THEY WERE HOLY ROLLERS! Can you imagine the vanity and human pride our Lord must contend with!

Each of them desperately wondered if Jesus Christ might do something for him. At the same time they were frightened to death that the Lord might reach out and touch them! It was an experience, one they talked about for weeks after the service. I explained to each man that he did not have to go anywhere. If he wanted to be taken to future services, we would go, BUT NOT AS A REQUIREMENT - AS A PRIVILEGE!

At later dates several of our residents went forward for help and in each case was "slain in the Spirit" for the first time in his life. Two asked to be taken to the Hunter Ministries' offices for private prayer, and the same thing happened. Their reaction can best be summed up by a telephone conversation I overheard a resident have with his Methodist brother. He said, "I DON'T KNOW WHAT THEY HAVE, BUT IT KNOCKED ME RIGHT FLAT ON MY BACK!" What a wonderful and sincere witness to the power of God!

This was my *first* meeting with a whole group of excited Christians!

CHAPTER 21
ABOUT WATER BAPTISM

I spent my early lifetime hearing arguments about the various forms of baptism, bitter words about who was and who was not "saved" because of his or her style of baptism. I hated all of it. These discussions were void of love and therefore void of God, because the Bible says "GOD IS LOVE."

I was sprinkled with a wet rose in some infant form of baptism and christening, but since I never got "worthy" enough for communion until I was in my forties, I also never felt qualified to discuss forms of baptism. Various relatives in various other churches bluntly told me I was going to hell because I lacked proper baptism. Since I had already made that commitment for myself, it didn't seem important. THEIR LACK OF LOVE AND TACT DID SEEM IMPORTANT. I think I really expected to run across them in a hot hereafter.

After my quiet conversion, baptism by immersion began to come to mind, without any suggestion from anyone. I still feel our Lord, in his mercy, kept all those waterlogged Christians away from me while he dealt with my mind personally.

When a mass water baptismal service came about I got right in the middle of it. No great healing or enlightenment came about at this time. No great emotional experience was had. I wasn't at all disappointed. I had quietly and definitely followed a personal leading. I did this outside my church, even though my church offers whatever form of baptism we request. My rector is a busy man with an eighteen-hour day, and I simply saved him time he could use elsewhere.

It was necessary for me to follow Jesus' baptism as closely as I could. We did pretty well - in a river on a hot Sunday afternoon - but for me it was a commitment to close the gap where religion often departs from Christianity! So I am now double baptized - by sprinkling in 1925 and by immersion in a river in 1974 - that's a long time between baptisms!

CHAPTER 22
ABOUT DELIVERANCE

I have had two major experiences with deliverance, and many other experiences with attitudes and feelings. My first deliverance experience was of a desire for alcohol. I had become a member of a helping fellowship which, I believe, is God-endowed for my kind of people. But I still knew that I would have trouble unless I lost a desire for drink. I got down on my knees by my bed and quietly talked to God about my need, telling him he knew all things, and stating, "You know I'll never make it without a deliverance from desire."

There were no flashes of light! There was no instant miracle of deliverance, but a couple of months later I discovered I HAD LOST ALL DESIRE TO DRINK. I do not even know when it happened, but I am, and always have been grateful to God for this major work in my life.

I did not possess great faith.

I did not "know God would do it." I knew he COULD do it for me, but I was not at all sure he would.

I cannot explain the miracle of deliverance from a desire for alcohol, BUT I DIDN'T NEED TO UNDERSTAND IT TO ENJOY THE MANY BENEFITS THESE MANY YEARS.

Because she had smoked five packs of cigarettes a day, Frances Hunter is death on smoking. She feels as keenly about the evil of smoking as I do about alcohol. When you've been there and back, there seems to be great opportunity for a hang-up, if you want to call it that.

I read her writings on smoking. I heard her talk about it and proclaim instant deliverance. I was curious. I had no great conviction on the sin of smoking. I did read the warning now placed on all cigarette packs, and I wanted to be free of a definite health hazard. I knew that being healthier and more energetic made better Christians. I knew God COULD give instant deliverance, but again, I was not sure he WOULD do it. I think I was still hung up on the old "unworthiness" bit.

So I brought nothing more than curiosity and hope to a meeting where the Hunters did their cigarette bit. I went forward with about forty other smokers. The Hunters moved very fast because of the number of people and the time required for the entire service. Charles was on my side of the building and I had wanted Frances because she had the experience of having smoked five packs a day and I smoked three and a half. I wasn't sure whether Charles had ever smoked and whether our Lord ever worked through teetotalers to "totalers" like me. While I was thinking all these thoughts, the fast movement came closer to me. I caught a glimpse of the lady on my right, a convent-educated Catholic, as she fell flat on her back as he touched her. By the time he had touched me quickly and lightly with a prayer of about four words, "Jesus, deliver my brother," an electric kind of force hit me, and I was flat on my back!

After a few minutes I got up, and I didn't feel very different. With my Irish logic, I thought, "This may be all well and good tonight in a church, but what about tomorrow at the house when all the residents light up a cigarette? Will I want one?" I had crushed the pack I brought and thrown it and my lighter into a trash can as a token of my desire and intention, but I still had a supply at home and in my car.

Would you believe that I went from three and one-half packs of cigarettes a day to none without any desire and without any nervous reaction at all? This was my very first experience of being knocked flat by an unusual power and of INSTANT DELIVERANCE FROM A THIRTY-YEAR HABIT. It was amazing! I enjoyed such painless freedom with NO EFFORT ON MY PART AT ALL! I even felt a bit guilty when friends were struggling with some self-discipline to quit smoking, and I had a free ride from the Lord.

I witnessed to everyone who would hold still long enough. "Didja' know that I had an instant deliverance from a three-and-a-half-pack a day, thirty-year smoking habit with just a four-word prayer - and that I was knocked flat on my back in the process?" This is pretty far-out witnessing to some of the wild people I still know in the world of entertainment and music! Since they all knew I was pretty far-out anyway, it was an easy witness. When you've been the biggest drunk in town and suddenly come up looking like Little Boy Blue, they come to expect anything. They also call you at three in the morning to ask how you did it!

DELIVERANCE IS REAL! NEVER DOUBT IT.

How and when God works is always amazing to me. We have had alcoholics who had everything going for them fail to get anything from God or seem to make any kind of contact. There have been others who crawled out from under a bridge and came out looking like St. John the Divine! I have no explanation. I also have no more questions for God. I am content that he DOES work. Knowing he is all wisdom, I am content with how and with whom he will work.

There have been other deliverances from attitudes of resentment and fear, the little daily miracles God does for us when we back up, shut up, and wait. I don't know about you French, English, and Swedish folks, but we Irish have great difficulty with BACKING UP, SHUTTING UP, AND WAITING ON THE LORD!

I have come to expect deliverances and miracles as a part of my daily experience, and they happen!

CHAPTER 23
A SPIRITUAL ILLNESS

What do you do when you find yourself with freedom and deliverance from alcohol and cigarettes. . .when one day you suddenly discover you don't drink, smoke, dance, gamble, commit adultery, or a maze of other "don'ts" pushed by most Christians? You may very well come down with a case of spiritual illness as I did! Being this pure can be dangerous! It can cause all kinds of complications if one isn't careful and close to the Lord in daily communion.

When I discovered just how perfect I was, I polished up my halo, dusted off my white robe, spread my wings, and climbed right up on the judgment seat! SINCE THE JUDGMENT SEAT IS RESERVED FOR GOD, I repeat, THIS CAN BE DANGEROUS! The seat is very high and you can fall a long, long way! Thank God for my shyness and reserve. At least I wasn't vocal about all this, but quietly and privately I began to judge all the other folks I knew and some I didn't know. I passed out my judgment on whether they smoked or drank, whether they prayed in tongues, whether they did, or did not, believe in or experience healing or deliverance. I judged who was, and was not, a believer in our Lord. I'm sure you've never done this, but you will be interested to know that I have. You may also be interested to learn what it costs to presume so much!

With all this quiet and silent judgment I began to notice that something drastic had happened to my Christian experience - that all the excitement and joy had gone out of it. I wondered why anyone as perfect as I was shouldn't have double doses of joy and peace every single day. After all, someone with as many miracle works in his life was indeed in close contact with God, and God owed me something in joy and peace.

I spent several months in this spiritual mess until I finally became alarmed at the change in my life. I was a child of God, but I didn't feel like a child of God. I HAD NO LOVE FOR MY NEIGHBOR, BUT I HAD A GREAT DEAL OF JUDGMENT FOR HIM!

Finally, in alarm and desperation, I went back to one of my very early alcoholic recovery prayers: LORD STRAIGHTEN ME OUT! In mercy, our Lord allowed me to stand in front of a huge full-length spiritual mirror and get a good look at myself. What I saw was what I had always hated the most in all the fundamental religionists I had ever known. I had become all this and more.

Here was a physically fat, puffed up, pompous, judgmental and prideful person who had no joy and no peace of mind. This view literally made me sick.

Weakly, after a long spiritual sickness, I climbed down off the judgment seat and gave it back to God. I made God a promise that if he would return my peace of mind, I would never again presume to judge anyone who smoked, drank, cussed, gambled, or slept with everyone in town! AND I MEANT IT! The loss of personal contact with God and the loss of personal peace is the loss of life for my kind of people. We cannot dabble around with basics and live. You who have never known the horrors of an alcoholic problem may be able to do all kinds of things and get away with it, but I can't and retain my safety with life itself.

I have regained the calm, quiet peace that was Jesus' promise to believers. I do not judge anyone, because I cannot afford to do so. IT COSTS TOO MUCH.

If you parade into church some Sunday stark naked, I will not judge you. I will assume God can temporarily blind everyone present or that he created the body and may have some purpose in exposing one of his creations. Is this a drastic attitude? NOT NEARLY AS DRASTIC AS THE ATTITUDE OF JUDGMENT!

CHAPTER 24
THE VALLEY OF THE SHADOW OF FAT!

About the same time I got involved with judgment and pride, I took up another bad habit. After all, if you don't drink, don't smoke, don't dance, don't gamble, etc., etc., etc.. . .you must do something! So I took up the number one Christian sin. I BEGAN TO EAT! I ate to make up for all the drinking, smoking, gambling and other uglies I didn't do. I ate whole pies, because I "needed the sugar in my dry, recovered, alcoholic condition." It had been many years since I had any alcohol, and I didn't need that sugar for anything. IT WAS BLATANT GLUTTONY AND NOTHING LESS.

I blamed it on not smoking. After all, one gains a few pounds when one stops smoking. One does not gain in excess of seventy pounds from not smoking. ONE GAINS THAT MUCH FROM OVEREATING. I had a weight problem because all my family had this problem. This was not true. They had a weight problem, not because they didn't smoke, didn't drink, didn't dance, didn't gamble and didn't do a lot of other things, BUT BECAUSE THEY ATE TO EXCESS!

Freedom in Christ does not mean that we are free to indulge ourselves in eating to excess to merely substitute for all the habits we scorn in others. THERE IS ABSOLUTELY NO DIFFERENCE IN ALCOHOLISM AND OVEREATING. Both need self-discipline, and both CAN KILL YOU! Neither make us good Christian witnesses.

I had to come face to face with the sin of overindulgence, and I had to do something about it.

It is not a sin to eat excess sweets? I wonder why I never did it in the presence of other people. I did it in secret, because I felt if nobody saw me, it didn't count. The end result was that SECRET EATING PUT ON PUBLIC FAT! I was in full view of everyone. I wasn't marching in the army of the Lord. I WAS WADDLING! One cannot march with that much excess weight.

It is time we all realized that our bodies are indeed the temple of the Holy Spirit, and fat temples are not nearly as effective! I have used every justification you can name, so I am up on all of yours. But if we face facts that our Christian witness and example is greatly harmed, if not entirely eliminated, we may get brutally honest enough to begin doing something about it!

I learned another startling fact! I cannot pray for God to do something about my excess weight WITH A BIBLE IN ONE HAND AND A SLICE OF CHEESECAKE IN THE OTHER! It is the same as with alcoholism. We find no alcoholic can pray with any degree of contact with a bottle still clutched in his hand. While I am being so honest, let's admit that there are very few "glandular problems" but a lot of glandular excuses! Incidentally, God heals glandular problems if you want to be a slim and trim witness for the Lord!

It is a shame when we can't get three Christians in one pew at a meeting because we have overstuffed ourselves. I don't know what you plan to do about it, but I backed my PRAYER with PERSONAL ACTION, and the results were amazing. I plan to be one of those skinny Christians and am well on the way! I feel better! I look better! I have all the energy I never had waddling about for the Lord! My body temple is going to retain a much better design and one that its Creator ordered in my life.

Do you want to know another thing? I never remember hearing very well in a service conducted by a fat minister! I know God can use anyone, but words about the discipline we need for the Christian life never seem to reach me FROM FAT LIPS!

CHAPTER 25
THE FRUIT EXPERTS

If I don't do any of the major sins and have replaced Christian eating with a kind of Quaker discipline, I may find new problems. I can't judge others, because that has been a disaster. I may skirt the sin of judgment and use another scripture which says, "Ye shall know them by their fruits." (Matt. 7:16) With this scripture I can go out and busy myself with becoming a "fruit expert," examining the crop on everyone else's tree! It is scriptural, and therefore it must be right. The only problem is that I find being a "fruit expert" is too similar to being a judge, and I feel that danger may be lurking as I check out the various fruits on the spiritual trees of various folks.

So I put down my blue ribbons and red ribbons and all the first and second and third prizes I had planned to give out. I go back and busy myself EXAMINING MY OWN TREE to see if I am producing any of those good fruits by which our spiritual status is known. I find myself sadly lacking in a great deal of the produce department. What do I do? I get busy pruning and cutting back and working with prayer and fasting and asking our Lord to produce something good for his use in my life. I am not a fruit expert for others, but I do need to look at some of my own produce. As I do make some more honest effort in my own experience, I find more peace and more joy are the result of that effort.

There seems to be so little difference between a "fruit expert" and a "judge" that I need to be very careful in my own experience lest I confuse the two. In all cases, if I am busy in my own life, I do not have much time to check out others!

CHAPTER 26
GOD HAS A SENSE OF HUMOR

I grew up with the idea that God was always scowling and always dead serious, just looking for any excuse to burn us up in hell. It took me years to learn that we are created in the image of God and therefore, the facets of our make-up also be the facets of his make-up, and this includes a sense of humor!

Many happenings have proven this fact to be true over the years, but one in particular stands out since it is one of the most recent.

With my realization that I had become a fat Christian there came a desire to do something about it, or rather to have God do something about it. Still thinking God ran the corner miracle store and catered to my whims, or was always ready to pull my fat out of the fire, I went for prayer for some instant and effortless weight loss. I had heard glowing tales of someone who had instant weight loss after prayer so that his pants fell down. I hoped to have something similar happen. Shy as I am about the public falling-down of my pants, I was willing to endure this rather than face the strict self-discipline required to help get me in shape.

Off I went, hoping the same instant miracle would solve my excess weight as had zapped the smoking habit!

In the privacy of an office, a minister did the "laying on of hands" and asked for a loss of fifty-eight pounds. I noticed the man doing the prayer was more than a bit rotund himself. I wondered why God hadn't slimmed him down a bit, just to help my faith in this matter. I waited for my pants to fall and the instant and effortless miracle to begin. It never happened! OH, HOW I WANTED THAT MIRACLE! It would really be something to witness to. INSTANT WEIGHT LOSS! I had noticed lately that when I witnessed about the instant smoking deliverance, people looked at my waistline and said, "How nice!" I knew the instant loss of weight would do it all! I waited on the Lord, and I ate more German chocolate pie. NOTHING HAPPENED! My pants did not fall down. THEY GOT TIGHTER!

It was then that I began to suspect that the Almighty God did not do instantly what we could, and should do for ourselves. I switched over to a more reasonable pray-and-weigh program, and the weight began to slip off. I passed right by Sara Lee cheesecake and reminded myself that I was going to be a skinny Christian, a better witness, and a better designed body temple of our Lord.

One day after a loss of some thirty-five pounds, I came out of the shower in my shorts to answer the telephone. There, in the privacy of my bedroom, my shorts silently and easily slid to the floor! It was as iff od said, "Okay, little child, if you want your pants to fall off from weight loss, here they go! And in the privacy of your own room." I have never had such a laugh! I got the desire of my heart, but with some effort on my part.

This and other incidents in my experience lead me to believe that God must laugh right out loud at some of our ideas about what we "need" and what we "want." In my case I needed some self-discipline and someppto put forth some effort. God has no corner miracle store for our every whim. HE HANDLES WHAT WE CANNOT HANDLE. He lets us handle what we can handle. It is a teamwork of the greatest order. Once we begin, he always meets us more than halfway!

CHAPTER 27
SOCIAL OUTREACH

I was shocked to learn that one of my city's largest churches has no social outreach ministry at all! If you are hungry or destitute, don't go there, because there is no such ministry to help you. A widow, who was a member of the congregation, lost her home because no helping ministry was available to her. THIS IS NOT A FULL GOSPEL. It is sadly lacking in what Jesus did and what he told us to do. It is plainly given in scriptural instruction. Jesus took care of the needs of the people as he went among them.

"Oh, but we might get mixed up with all kinds of bums and low-class people," is the cry. Jesus got mixed up with sinners, publicans, tax collectors, and prostitutes, and it did not seem to bother his ministry. Indeed, it was a large part of it. I know there are good governmental social organizations to take care of such situations. BUT THE COMMISSION WAS NOT GIVEN TO THE GOVERNMENT OR THE RED CROSS. It was given to Christians like you and me and the congregations we make up who call ourselves "Christian."

So we get mixed up with some bums and some lower-class people...we might also ENTERTAIN SOME ANGELS UNAWARE! We could all do with a bit of angelic entertaining!

Outreach is constant! It is daily. IT IS OFTEN TIRING! I have been weary many times from the needs of others. I have been used many times by the earth's users. But our Lord didn't say, "Love your neighbor as yourself if he doesn't try to use you." He just said I was to love my neighbor as myself. Is it easy? It certainly is not. In fact, it is humanly impossible to get THAT involved with the needs of others, but when I feel human weakness coming on, I pray again, and ask for the love of God to pour THROUGH me to others. I find it always does. I go on and love remains, because it is given to me. You may say, "The first and great commandment is to love God with all our heart and mind and soul." This is true, but the second commandment is almost like it, and on these two commandments hang ALL the law and the prophets. I find I cannot do the first UNLESS I CAN ALSO DO THE SECOND!

Since I work in alcoholic recovery I am often in the clubs and meeting rooms of Alcoholics Anonymous. On the wall of each meeting room I notice a sign which says, "WHENEVER ANYONE ANYWHERE REACHES OUT FOR HELP, I WANT THE HAND OF AA ALWAYS TO BE THERE, AND FOR THAT I AM RESPONSIBLE." I like that bold statement of obligation, and I have come to believe that we need to paraphrase it in the Christian experience.

We might say WHENEVER ANYONE ANYWHERE REACHES OUT FOR HELP, I WANT THE GOSPEL OF JESUS CHRIST ALWAYS TO BE THERE, AND FOR THAT I AM RESPONSIBLE. If we make it a "reality" expression we could turn the world around the other way! Imagine each Christian assuming RESPONSIBILITY for the Gospel at a *personal* level. And did you know that whether we state it or not, WE ARE RESPONSIBLE?

Ministers who preach sermons on the reality of a judgment day seem to harp on an accounting of what we did which was sinful. I often wonder if more emphasis shouldn't be placed on our sins of omission; our failure to do what we are required to do! Sometimes our failure to do anything at all!

Responsibility isn't easy. It is often difficult. But it is a vital part of my Christian experience and I can't escape it. I no longer want to escape it.

Did you ever stop to think that in many areas of our activities WE ARE THE ONLY BIBLE SOME PEOPLE WILL READ! They will look at us if we are a professing

Christian, and they will read our walking and living example because it is all they can handle at the time. Realizing this, can't we be a bit more active in living our Christianity? Shouldn't we let them see joy, peace, love, and compassion alive in our actions as an example of what Christianity is all about?

The Buick Automobile Company at one time had a slogan which I always remember. It said, ASK THE MAN WHO OWNS ONE. Isn't this the best test of the seeker who is looking for some answers in his troubled life and thinks Jesus Christ just may be that answer? If he asks the man who has the Christian experience, can we afford to look like we are struggling with some distasteful self-discipline which hurts and brings no joy? I think we need a little zap of the Holy Spirit and a zoom of the reality of Jesus in our lives so that we can sparkle a bit for the curious public. Now I don't mean a "goodie-goodie" Christian performance presenting ourselves as plaster saints who "gave up" this or that trait or habit. Man, they don't judge us on what we gave up... THEY JUDGE US ON WHAT WE'VE GOT! So if we've got something, let's let it glimmer a little or keep in such close contact with God that we can't turn it off!

Now don't rush out and make a study of the Christian you most admire and try to copy some style. BE YOURSELF! But be your most alive Christian self.

Perhaps some of us keep our Christianity very quiet because we have nothing to show for it. In that case we need to get down on our knees and pray asking Jesus to PUT A LITTLE ZIP IN OUR EXPERIENCE. There is no such thing as a Christian who is not obvious. We are all obvious to someone, either by what we have in our experience or what we do not have. I have come to believe my Christianity is not a private matter. I am witnessing all the time. I am "on" as they say in show business whether I plan to be on or not.

If I AM RESPONSIBLE for my constant state of witnessing and living my Christianity, then you must be also. We must all be responsible for how we look, how we act, how much joy we display, or how much peace shows in our faces.

So let's get with it Christians! Ladies, as you go to the supermarket you may be read by someone as you shop at the lettuce and tomato display. So let's zoom along with that extra zip that comes from a personal encounter with Jesus Christ. Gentlemen, as you work in your office, your employees or customers should know you are a Christian. Your actions may be the only Bible they will read for this time, and your life will speak of your experience to someone. Let's live it up a little and show what we have, or get busy getting it if we don't have it yet! Remember, they had to cover Moses' face with a cloth when he came down from the mountaintop encounter with God. Maybe they won't need to cover us up, but I think we should all glow a little bit from our contact with the Lord! And for that, I am responsible.

CHAPTER 28

THE CHARISMATIC MOVEMENT

Much is said today about the "Charismatic Movement." To be in it or out of it, for it or against it, seems to be the order of the day. Nobody really seems to know how it all began or where. It seems terribly important to some people to sanction it, and to others to disapprove. The workings of Almighty God do not need mere man's approval or disapproval. THEY WILL GO ON VERY WELL WITHOUT IT.

Cliques and groups do not seem in order. We cannot reach others if we withdraw from them into some little group. The real meaning of the Charismatic Movement seems to be a simple realization that the gifts of the Holy Spirit including healing and deliverance are very real! This has been happening with such regularity to so many believers and seekers from such varied spiritual backgrounds that only God could bridge such gaps and borders!

It is not a place to go, so much as a way of living and thinking and believing. It is simply the grace of God drawn near to a man who opens up to believe and receive it.

There is a kinship among those who experience such unusual spiritual graces. There is an immediate recognition among such people. I never need ask those in our church if they have received the baptism of the Holy Spirit. I have an instant inner spiritual witness which tells me exactly what has happened in their lives. I tried at one time to "get in" groups and locations which offered experiences similar to my own, but the Lord wouldn't let me. When I am led to remain in my congregation and worship with such peace in a traditional way, I must assume that God has some real purpose in it. I am completely content. My experience has been that I am not in the Charismatic Movement. THE CHARISMATIC MOVEMENT IS IN ME!

CHAPTER 29

A MORE EXCELLENT WAY

Are you an alcoholic? Do you have a drinking problem? Are you a drunk? Maybe you think you "just drink a little too much?" Whatever one calls it, the end result is the same - TROUBLE AND MORE TROUBLE!

Perhaps you've already tried all the known programs including AA. AA is a very spiritual program; the thing you may need first of all is a SPIRITUAL EXPERIENCE to work it.

The only reason I've written this book is to share my experience in the hope of showing to others that there is SALVATION, DELIVERANCE, HELP AND HOPE THROUGH JESUS CHRIST.

Perhaps someone is reading this who isn't struggling with the problem of alcohol. Yours may be a problem of a far different nature. It doesn't matter to Jesus! Salvation is freely given and it's available to anyone who wants it. The Apostle Paul wrote: "For all have sinned, and come short of the glory of God." (Rom. 3:23) Notice that word ALL...that excludes no one. You don't have to be an alcoholic to qualify! To "fall short" means we don't measure up to God's glorious ideal. But this is not a do-it-yourself program.

Paul goes on to assure us that God did something about this impossible situation: "Yet now God declares us 'not guilty' of offending him if we trust in Jesus Christ, who in his kindness freely takes away our sins." (vs. 24 TLB) There's only one little word that stands between you and God and release from sin. That little word is IF..."IF we trust in Jesus Christ."To turn away from that is to reject KINDNESS FREELY GIVEN. "For God sent Christ

Jesus to take the punishment for our sins and to end all God's anger against us." (vs. 25a TLB)

IT IS SUCH A BEAUTIFUL OFFER AND LASTS FROM HERE THROUGH ALL ETERNITY. "For salvation that comes from trusting Christ. . .is within easy reach of each of us; in fact, it is as near as our own hearts and mouths. For if you tell others with your own mouth that Jesus Christ is your Lord, and believe in your own heart that God has raised him from the dead, you will be saved. For it is by believing in his heart that a man becomes right with God; and with his mouth he tells others of his faith, confirming his salvation. For the Scriptures tell us that no one who believes in Christ will ever be disappointed. . .Anyone who calls upon the name of the Lord will be saved." (Rom. l0:8-10, 13 TLB)

Let me assure you that if you believe in your heart as these Scriptures so clearly show, that Jesus Christ will do what the Word declares. JESUS CHRIST STILL WORKS MIRACLES OF DELIVERANCE TODAY. *You* can have that DELIVERANCE right where you are and right now!

If you are an alcoholic, a drunk, or someone who "just drinks a little too much," the first step is to put down the bottle, or better yet, pour it out as an ACTION ON YOUR PART that you are not kidding and that you do mean business with God. Now, RELAX a bit. Take a deep breath of the Lord's good air. Have you seen the little plaque which hangs on many walls all over this world? It says simply, "LET GO AND LET GOD!" There's the secret. . . RELAX AND LET GO of the problem with alcohol. You've already learned you can't handle it and that you get into trouble with it. So let go of this thing you can't handle.

Now, with a simple and sincere prayer comes the next part. . .LET GOD! Here's a suggested prayer:
> "Father God, this alcoholic problem is too big for me. I cannot handle it. So I LET GO OF IT. I am now willing to LET YOU TAKE THE DESIRE FOR ALCOHOL AWAY FROM ME. I ask

for a HEALING of this addictive illness. This problem is IMPOSSIBLE for me. But WITH YOU, ALL THINGS ARE POSSIBLE. I ask for this HEALING in the name of Jesus Christ. Amen."

If your problem is other than alcohol, substitute cigarettes, bad attitudes, or whatever your deliverance need, and pray that prayer sincerely. Then apply the following added suggestions.

Pray this prayer over and over again if you need to do so. Pray it until you get an answer and know that there is a change in your heart and mind. DELIVERANCE IS REAL. NEVER DOUBT IT.

Now, if your problem *is* alcohol, you will be able to understand and work the twelve suggested steps of Alcoholics Anonymous. They are all deeply spiritual steps, and deliverance is a deeply spiritual experience.

NEVER UNDERESTIMATE THE VALUE OF A SPIRITUAL FOLLOW-UP PROGRAM TO CLEAR AWAY THE WRECKAGE OF YOUR PAST LIFE SO THAT YOU ARE NEVER TROUBLED BY IT AGAIN.

If you should have the return of a desire to drink, use a simple prayer like this:

"Father, I LET GO of this problem. It is no longer mine, but it is YOURS. I ASK YOU TO REMOVE THE DESIRE. Amen."

Keep using this prayer until you suddenly find the desire no longer remains. In some cases the desire never returns after the first prayer. In other cases there may be a few times of returning temptation. I do not know why, and this is God's business, but I do know that a simple prayer is the greatest weapon we can use. IT CAN ALWAYS WORK!

Let me warn you that you cannot experience deliverance from alcoholism and THEN SIT IDLY DOING NOTHING. GET BUSY! GET INVOLVED! Get into an AA group. Get involved with some church or spiritual group. It is both scriptural and practical to get busy. "Idle hands are the devil's workshop" was never more true than with the recovering alcoholic. Remember, God does not deliver us so that we can drink like "normal" people! He delivers us so that we no longer have a need to drink at all! Talk to God about ALL your problems. Talk to him like a close friend over the back yard fence. EXPECT CHANGES in your life from these talks!

I do not pretend in these short essays to give the impression that I have all the answers for the Christian experience. I want just to share what I have learned thus far. I still see through a glass darkly. There is still much I need to know, still a long way to go. This experience is a lifetime of learning and growing. I often think if I live to be five hundred I'll still only begin to understand how much I don't know!

The daily walk, the little answers for each day, and the larger answers and deliverances and healings, make this such a fascinating adventure that I just had to share some of it with you. IT IS INDEED A MORE EXCELLENT WAY!

CHAPTER 30
BOOM BOOM RAZZMATAZZ RELIGION!

For everything that is real there is a counterfeit, and the Christian experience is no exception. Much of what is done today on the fringes of the spiritual revolution is as phony as pink mink! And much is as genuine as milk and honey! It is our inner spirit which gives warning as to what is real and what is not. When our inner spirit is controlled by the Holy Spirit, we can know what God is doing as distinguished from man's mimicking mutterings.

I have found some safeguards to misleading religious performances as opposed to real spiritual worship experience. The Holy Spirit always comes from the INSIDE TO THE OUTSIDE, and never from the outside to the inside. If I must be worked up to an emotional high pitch in order to gain some spiritual excitement, then it is an emotional binge and not a spiritual experience. There is probably nothing wrong with emotional binges if you like that sort of thing. But they do tend to leave one exhausted, whereas a real inner spiritual worship experience leaves one in great peace. I have seen both, and I have experienced both. I much prefer the real spiritual worship experience.

It is not the volume but the attitude of the heart which makes the contact with God in worship.

I am not putting down the making of a "joyful noise unto the Lord" in whatever degree of loudness it may produce. Heaven will be full of praises to God and I do not believe these will be soft whispers of praise.

I have been greatly blessed and have worshipped with great volume in my own church when trumpets were blaring and the organ and choir were going full blast in praise to the Lord. But what I am trying to say is that in-between the joy and loudness of our praise, I personally find a refueling and refilling process in the SILENT time when I am so completely in awe of the greatness of God that there is no possible way to express it but to sit in silence waiting for that still small voice within.

As our experience with Jesus Christ and his reality goes deeper, our volume of praise often goes higher AND I AM ALL FOR IT!

But when you are finished worshipping God with praises and shouts of joy, do try the silent time and experience the wonders that this waiting before the Lord can bring into your life and your Christian experience. Like the man said, TRY IT! YOU'LL LIKE IT!

I am not especially conservative. I grew up in a church with much noise and little forgiveness. I can rattle and bang with the best of them! But I have already had all I want that is not real. I seek only what IS real. When I say, "PRAISE THE LORD!" I prefer it to be a whisper that wells up from inside, rather than a shout that is done simply because it seems to be the thing to say! You may be just the opposite and need a spiritual boost by a joyful noise unto the Lord.

Perhaps the hardest thing for any of us to do is to be still and wait upon the Lord. The Bible says, "BE STILL, AND KNOW THAT I AM GOD." I fear we are often so busy and so noisy that we take no time to be still. I understand the Society of Friends Church, or the Quakers, have a part of their worship service that is called "The Silence." It is a time in which they wait upon the Lord in complete and total silence. I like this form of worship. I believe we might make more contact with God if we adopted it into some of our worship time.

Perhaps if we got still and silent and waited more often, God might be more able to speak to us in the depths of our hearts on matters of great importance to our spiritual growth and well-being.

I'm not judging any form of worship. I am simply stating my own experience in learning the simplicity of silence and to "Be still, and know that I am God."

I think it might be wise to wedge this in somewhere between the blaring of the trumpets and the clanging of the tambourines! Next time you are in trouble, and we all get into trouble, try refraining from chanting to our Lord all your problems. He knows what you have need of before you ask. Just sit in perfect silence and be still before the Lord. Listen! Some new and fantastic solutions to those problems may come your way before you even ask. You may discover, as I did, a new depth and spiritual peace from just BEING SILENT BEFORE OUR GOD.

I am not suggesting that we all adopt a formal form of worship which suggests a casket may roll down the aisle at any moment, but I am asking if we may not be so noisy and busy at times that God could not be heard in a "still, small voice" if he spoke to us! (see I Kings 19:12, 13)

CHAPTER 31

DIGNITY WITH POWER

> "...HAVING A FORM OF GODLINESS, BUT DENYING THE POWER THEREOF: FROM SUCH TURN AWAY." (II Tim. 3:5)

The Charismatics have such POWER!
The traditional Church has such DIGNITY!
Oh, for the day when the traditional Church has more POWER,
And the Charismatics have more DIGNITY.
But, in the meantime, if I must make a choice, I'll take the Charismatics and the POWER!
I CAN GET GREAT DIGNITY WHEN I ATTEND THE OPERA!

CHAPTER 32
A LITTLE AND A LOT

Almost everything I do revolves around my work with recovering alcoholics. I find the parallels of recovery and the growth in Christianity so close that the principles are interchangeable. What works for recovery works in spiritual growth. What works in spiritual growth works also in recovery.

One of our recovery therapy projects is gardening. We use it both for the produce and for teaching principles. It is what you PUT IN the earth that governs what you GET OUT of it. I find this true in Christian experience. Such phrases as, "Give, and it shall be given unto you," and "Forgive us our trespasses as we forgive those who trespass against us," take on a divine principle of action and movement which I cannot and do not ignore.

I can look back on a life of "nothing" and see where my crop was planted by me. "Nothing" was happening in my life because it was "nothing" that I planted. Nothing grows into nothing.

I can look back on other times of misery and chaos and see that I planted, watered, and grew all the misery myself. It was my crop and I had to harvest it. Whether it is a garden or our lives, we get out of it only what we put in with the multiplying growth added.

If I want big sunflowers in my life then I had better not plant seeds of tiny daisies. I get only what I plant. If I want to receive in my life, then I plant the process by giving. Only what I invest will make a return. It is simple, direct, and easy to understand. Never a harvest without planting, watering, and cultivating.

This simple, childlike principle is too obvious to really need mentioning, but like all late-blooming plants, it was all new to me - late, but not too late.

In my work with alcoholics I can tell you who will make a real recovery and who will not almost by the end of a week at our facility. I look to see who is getting involved in the project, the house, garden, repair, and maintenance of our equipment and facilities. Those who are planting seeds in activity will make an excellent recovery, find new contacts with God, and experience wonderful things in life. Those who are not planting and working in an area of opportunity will not do so good. Why? Because we get out of anything only the multiplied seeds we put into it. If we put nothing in, then when God multiplies that "nothing," we have a lot more of nothing. "For if you give, you will get! Your gift will return to you in full and overflowing measure, pressed down, shaken together to make room for more, and running over. Whatever measure you use to give - large or small - will be used to measure what is given back to you." (Luke 6:38 TLB)

Did you ever try such a simple thing as smiling on a first encounter with a stranger? Doesn't he usually return that smile? Perhaps it grows as he smiles at someone else and they take it on and on through the day.

Did you ever try planting seeds of Christian kindness on a busy freeway during the rush hour? Try it and see how it grows into something. You may find a totally new experience. Do you know what I do on a busy freeway in a rush of traffic? I smile at the occupants of other cars and bless them with the sign of the cross in the name of the Father, the Son, and the Holy Spirit. Do you know what they do when I bless them? They are so stunned, so blessed, or whatever happens, that they get clear out of my way and I move on in peace and ease just like on a country lane. Next time you are on a busy freeway and everyone looks as if they hate everyone else, try it. Bless all the people in all the cars which crowd you, and see if that blessing is not returned many times over in plenty of room to move along in traffic. Can you imagine the chain reaction of those whom we bless? Can't you just hear someone at home saying,"You know what happened to me on the freeway coming home? I was next to this funny-looking little man who smiled and blessed me and I couldn't help but smile all the way home!"

I do not question reactions or results, I just do my own thing and move along in our Lord's perfect peace. Try planting joy and peace on the freeway and see what happens. A whole new dimension in Christian driving may open up to you!

"Be not deceived; God is not mocked: for whatsoever a man soweth, that shall he also reap." (Gal. 6:7) We need all be keenly aware of this law of God. Let's plant with new concern. Let's be aware that we put in a little and get a little, or we put in a lot and get a lot. We have our own little department of agriculture and the Lord's crop insurance so we can't go wrong.

Plant some seeds in your church or parish. Plant more in some area of Christian ministry. See if your harvest bins don't overflow with more than you can handle in joy, peace, contentment, happiness, and the real "zing" our lives are meant to have.

CHAPTER 33

INVOLVEMENT - JESUS' STYLE

In Matthew 25:35 Jesus said: "For I was hungry, and ye gave me food; I was thirsty, and ye gave me drink; I was a stranger, and ye took me in; naked, and ye clothed me; I was sick, and ye visited me; I was in prison, and ye came unto me." Read the rest of that chapter and see if you get the wallop that I did.

This speaks to me loud and clear about Christian involvement. It says to me that I cannot truly love God without loving my fellowman. I can do nothing for God without doing it for my fellowman. To me it speaks of the brotherhood of man in the family of God, and ties it all together in such a way that I cannot escape it.

This gives me instruction for Christian outreach. This is meeting needs at the level of need (isn't that what Jesus always did?). This is witnessing in a practical way - or whatever else you wish to call it.

If I feed someone, I do so as unto the Lord. If I give a man a drink of water when he is thirsty, I do it as unto the Lord. If I take a stranger in, I do it as unto the Lord. This puts a whole new emphasis on involvement and the witness of "action Christians" in a very real and down-to-earth way.

No, you don't have to do it this way if you feel no need to do so. But, if I understand it as a very genuine and tangible expression of Christian love, then I must do it with all I have. If I believe it, then I must live it.

I have been deeply involved with this idea for many years, and there is no way to share the reality of the joy which comes from sharing in this manner. For me it has nothing at all to do with "social work" or "do-gooding."

It is a realization that what I do in the area of human need is done as unto our Lord Jesus Christ. There is unexplainable joy in the process. This is involvement - Jesus' style.

In Luke's Gospel, chapter ten (vss. 30-37), Jesus gives the parable of the good Samaritan. Here is another example of the way Jesus wants us to be involved in helping people. But I am amazed at the number of Christians who seem to think the good Samaritan was an insurance adjuster! If we think so, we need to go back and read it all again to get a true picture of what happened, and how it was done. Above all, we need to realize who was telling the story - JESUS - and why he was telling it. If Jesus taught with parables (earthly stories with a heavenly meaning), then he had a reason for the stories. I am trying to learn what to do and when and how to do it from these simple teachings of our Lord.

It has not always been easy. But then nobody said it would be. Sometimes people take advantage of my effort to share. Does this mean I should stop sharing just because some people use me without receiving the message? I think not. Do you realize Jesus Christ was used by people? Once he outright told a large group that they were following him for the loaves and fishes and free food and not for the Gospel he was teaching. Things haven't changed too much in two thousand years and often we, too, deal with the "free food" people. Jesus didn't stop sharing or teaching just because some of the people lacked in sincerity and their motives were subject to question.

It is my understanding that I am to share and, therefore, it becomes my responsibility. It is NOT my responsibility to ascertain the exact attitude of the person to whom I give and with whom I share.

For me, CHRISTIANITY IS A GIVING EXPERIENCE, as best demonstrated in John 3:16, "For God so loved the world, THAT HE GAVE HIS ONLY BEGOTTEN SON, that whosoever believeth in him should not perish, but have everlasting life."

As Christians, we can give and share in a variety of ways; but it will be vastly different as God uses us each in our own realm of service and influence. This is the beauty of real born-again-turned-on Christians as opposed to shriveled-up-dead-on-the-vine religionists. There is an area of responsibility for each of us, and the best way I know where to find it is to seek God's direction in sincere prayer.

Sometimes we are not directly involved with a ministry, but many people are used of the Lord as a back-up force to supply the needs of an action group. THIS IS INVOLVEMENT. THIS IS SHARING in a real way. In both prayer and material gifts, we are a definite part of the action.

No army can go out and win a battle without a munitions factory back of them with supplies. This is involvement of first-rate order. So if you have no direct involvement with meeting needs, outreach, ministry, or other action, ask the Lord to place you in a spiritual supply depot for those who are. The rewards are just as great although the actual contact is lacking. Very few Christian organizations and action groups could carry on without such back-up prayer and involvement on the part of the behind-the-scenes-type-people. Let me tell you that your life will be richer for getting involved Jesus' style. New joy will flood your soul.

Did you know that the Lord can bless you in wonderful ways when you are answering a telephone or stuffing envelopes for the cause of Christ? He can and does! I once had a ball answering telephone calls for my church on a Sunday morning! Stuffing envelopes or typing a mailing list for the annual budget can be a rewarding and necessary kind of involvement. This helps keep the church of Jesus Christ going. Without the inspiration of the Holy Spirit moving people into positions of action, the church or any ministry would not go on. But do it as unto the Lord (see Col. 3:23), and do it as the Word suggests - heartily (that means with enthusiasm!).

Involvement in the action of the Christian adventure is a must for anyone wanting to experience ALL the joy of the Lord!

Feed the hungry. Clothe the naked. Give a thirsty man a drink. Answer a telephone. Stuff an envelope. Send a check to back up what you believe in. It's all CHRISTIANITY IN ACTION. Warning: Don't expect applause or citations from friends when you get involved. My experience has been the opposite from some friends who view my work and the change in me. They say, "How can you live like this?" And I keep wondering what I am missing if I am really missing anything. There are people so outspoken about my work with alcoholics that they say, "You are crazy." And my answer is always the same, "Maybe I am. But I am happy. Are you?" And you know, I also seem to remember some things Jesus said as he gathered the disciples together around him and seated himself on the side of a mountain. He saw the multitudes - that says needy people to me - and then taught his disciples setting before them the perfect standard of righteousness. Included in those "blessed attitudes" (more often referred to as The Beatitudes) are these words, "Blessed are the merciful; for they shall obtain mercy" (read all of Matt. 5:1-12). It all comes back to involvement - Jesus' style.

CHAPTER 34

GOD'S MOVING COMPANY

Now that Christianity has rubbed holes in my religion, let's move from hole-y religion to workable Christianity without loopholes.

In the book of St. Matthew, in the middle of Chapter 17, verse 20, Jesus told his followers, "If ye have faith as a grain of mustard seed, ye shall say unto this mountain, Remove hence to yonder place; and it shall remove; and nothing shall be impossible unto you."

Can you imagine it? Moving mountains with so little equipment?

He said it could be done. I believe it!

Suppose we don't really need to move mountains around. Suppose we just need to move a few hills. Everyone has some mountains and some hills of "impossibility" in his life. We all face some of those situations where we can't climb over and we can't get under, and we haven't the time or strength to go around our mountains of difficulty.

What about the mustard seed equipment Jesus mentioned? He said it takes just a little bitty mustard seed size faith to get the mountain out of the way so we can move along. Maybe you think it was just a nice saying and it doesn't really work. OH, YES, IT DOES WORK! Faith as a grain of mustard seed can move a mountain quicker than you can say "Amen."

I have been seeing them moved for several years now and am anxious to tell you about what's been happening - great big mountains of difficulty and smaller hills of bother. They all move and they are not long in doing so.

No, I don't do it. IT'S THE LORD'S MOVING COMPANY doing the work. I just flash my little badge of mustard seed faith and take my stand as a child of God and then watch the old mountain begin to get out of my way. PRAISE THE LORD, IT DOES WORK. I have seen extreme difficulty vanish and the "impossible happen when I use this short prayer: "LORD, YOU HANDLE THIS. IT'S TOO BIG FOR ME."

Please don't stand there staring at the mountain, asking God why it has to be in your way. Experience the joy of mountain moving and get into a regular habit of seeing the Almighty God in daily living. All it takes is a little bit of faith. If you've never seen a single mustard seed, take the time to go to your local seed store and look at one. This will fix in your mind the smallness of the mustard seed's size, and make the statement of Jesus more real to you.

Look this teaching up in the Bible. Make the promise in Matthew 17:20 a part of your thinking. Read it over and over again until the reality of this message becomes a part of you. Then make the promise a reality by putting it into practice.

Got a mountain blocking your progress and forward movement? Well, don't just stand there, DO SOMETHING. Flash your badge! Show your birth certificate! Stand on the promise of our Lord! Stake your claim! Call on God's moving company and see the miracle in your life.

Read the instructions. Look them up in the Bible. When you get the message, USE IT! It is all a part of God's package deal for which we praise him!

CHAPTER 35

WHY SERENITY FARM, INC.?

Serenity Farm, Inc. is the name of the organization through which we minister healing recovery from alcoholism to all who reach that point of seemingly impossible return. Through Jesus they find an experience toward happy alcoholic and spiritual recovery. This organization is chartered by the State of Texas and approved as a tax exempt organization by the Internal Revenue Service of the United States. At the time of this writing it operates from a city dwelling, but the ultimate plans are for a farm.

The idea of removing problem people to a country setting is quite literally scriptural to me. We read in the Bible that we should "BE STILL, AND KNOW THAT I AM GOD." I believe this to be vital to the first reality contact with our Lord. Certainly one might be still in almost any location, but if location is of such little importance, why not hold a prayer group meeting in a downtown "Go-Go" joint? Why not? Because it is not the right place or atmosphere for the God contact we seek and need in a prayer group.

This project has worked in both the country and the city, but we find the results far better in a setting away from the concrete jungles, in a quiet place where a resident can stop running long enough to find that GOD IS, and where the totality of his being depends on his contact with God

Over a hundred years ago, General William Booth founded the Salvation Army when he discovered that a man could hear the Gospel of Jesus Christ much better if he was not hungry for food. We find that same Gospel can reach the ear of any alcoholic when the stress of city living is removed and he is in a quiet place with time to think, consider, accept, and pray. On a farm, I have seen the stress lines fade from a new resident's face in from five to seven days. They look from five to ten years younger. When the stress of the city is gone, then we get down to the basics of deliverance and freedom from alcoholism.

I once had a man ask me, "How do I find God as you have found him and understand him?"

My answer was "You will not find God as 'I' understand him, but you will find him as 'YOU' understand him, and as he reveals himself to you and becomes real in your life." I then made a suggestion that the man take a walk through the woods and keep an open mind, asking God to reveal himself. As he went toward the woods I asked our Lord to especially reveal himself to the seeking resident. Know what happened? The man got his own revelation of God and made his beginning. It was not my doing or his becoming a carbon copy of my experience, but it was by finding something real and vital for himself. God, as I understand him, may be of no value to the resident at all, but the personal contact with Jesus as he is met by the individual can and does work the miracles we seek!

Christianity in the country is not a new idea. It is not even my own. But I have been so led toward this goal that all else has paled and faded as a result of this leading. How God handles it all is not my concern. That he does handle it and will is my absolute belief. We do what we can to share with the resident and we pray.

When we don't know what to do, we pray.

When we have said it all and there seems to be no response, we pray.

When we get difficult people, we pray.

When we face a person with indifference, we pray.

And do you know what happens? God answers prayer in the most unusual ways.

I recall in past days that street meetings were used as a means of spreading the Gospel of our Lord. They were excellent and far-reaching in results. Stories of people who first heard the Gospel from a street preacher abound and they are very real. Who knows the far-reaching results of such evangelism! It is fantastic to hear of the zeal and boldness of such missions for the Lord.

There are many places to witness and many places to carry the message. But for our work and for our people who are sick in body, mind, and soul, I prefer a farm setting where it is quiet and peaceful, and where there is an opportunity to be still and know that God exists.

If you read your Bible, you will learn that Jesus withdrew from the crowds very often and many times he could not be found. He went to a garden to pray shortly before his arrest, trial and crucifixion. This suggests to me that a withdrawing to a secluded and quiet place may be the beginning of a great and new experience for those who desperately need one, to those who are going through their trial with a destitute death facing them.

Aside from the scriptural instruction to BE STILL, AND KNOW THAT I AM GOD, the country setting offers a place to work with hands in growing and learning the wonders of God's creation. We have long known that nature is a healer of stress for the human mind.

In the country a distressed man can gain back his pride by growing the food on his table, by cultivating the soil, by building barns or fences, or rooms so others may be cared for. By sharing his abilities and knowledge with other residents in a Christian community of love in action, he can give as it has been given to him.

Above all, I believe in the reality of Serenity Farm because the Lord has never allowed me to escape the idea of what we are supposed to do in this setting. I have reached a peace in my heart where I no longer wish to escape the idea. I look forward with full confidence that God has his "Serenity Farm" picked out - a place where God can grow reality Christians from what appears to be bad seed. A place to be quiet and alone with God without fearing God. A place where we finally learn that God is love and he is the only solution to our problems. A place to take troubled people and let them literally come apart and be separate from the world for awhile.

We take in "impossible" people and turn out solid citizens, strong in the deliverance and protection of the Almighty God. Does it work? YES, IT WORKS WITHOUT FAILURE. If any man or woman sincerely seeks freedom from alcoholism, then he or she will get that freedom. If he or she is not sincere in a desire for change, nobody can help them. God never forces a miracle. HE GIVES TO THOSE WHO SEEK.

CHAPTER 36

LUNCH WITH A MIRACLE

I just had lunch with a miracle!

This man was "impossible" five years ago. He came to us with almost nothing except a little hope. He said, "Something told me to come here." That "something" was Almighty God and he turned this man's world upside down.

It was amazing to sit there and talk with this miracle man and literally see a new creature in Christ. To talk of the old things that have passed away and the wonder of all things made new. To remember in mental flashbacks how he looked then and how he looks now. How he acted then and how he acts now. How he felt then and how he feels now. And how he talked then and how much he has changed. I do not think this man is even aware of the tremendous change in his life in every area of his being.

When he came to us someone called me on the phone to tell me not to waste my time with the man; that he had been everywhere for help already and that he was one of the "impossible people" in alcoholic recovery. I thanked the caller and assured him my time is never wasted and only God can say who is and is not impossible.

We went to work on the problems of addiction. We went to work on the reality of the Gospel of Jesus Christ. Let me tell you that God went to work on the individual and the results are not over yet. Such a change you would not believe! This is not some do-it-yourself program. It is the grace of God in action today and for right now! If someone tells you it all stopped with the last of the original Apostles, don't you believe it. Impossible things are happening every day. My business card boldly states, I BELIEVE IN MIRACLES. I AM ONE! And remember that I am not an isolated case of God's re-creation.

My luncheon companion was without hope five years ago with one exception. He had a personal encounter with our Lord and you know what happened then! If you don't know, PLEASE do find out for yourself. Today this same man who had nothing has a lovely wife, a beautiful home, two cars, an excellent job, and is standing tall in the community with that special serenity and security which comes from God.

He is busy and involved in active Christianity and the needs of the community. But do you know how he spends his spare time? Coming here to Serenity Farm to witness of his experience and to share with our residents what has happened in his life. He uses his accounting abilities without pay for our work, and shares in so many ways that time and space do not allow me to tell it properly.

This is Christianity in action. This is the reality of Jesus Christ lighting up the world in the faces of people whose expressions were not so bright and cheerful a few years ago. Praise the Lord for his mercy and goodness to us!

If you think the luncheon date was a single experience let me quickly tell you that I had coffee with another miracle just this week. This was a four-year miracle but just as much aglow as a brightly lit Christmas tree!

Again the same experience. A new creature who has been literally reborn and does not even look like the same man who came to us shaking and sick four years ago. He is NOT the same man!

This same man came with so little, and I recall how we all laughed when he managed to buy a car for thirty-five dollars. You should see his car today! And you should meet his lovely wife. You would enjoy holding his new baby boy. You would be interested to know that he owns a good part of his business and is doing very well. You also might like to visit him in his beautiful new home. HOW DID THIS CHANGE TAKE PLACE? He came to believe that God could and would help him if he sought God. He sought and found, and the windows of heaven opened up, and he seems to be still trying to catch up on the counting of blessings.

Please understand that we simply provided care and an atmosphere where a needy person can seek and find God as he understands him. It was God's doing. We do not deal in "religion." We share the hope of real, genuine Christianity and then watch the miracle happen.

Exciting? Yes, it certainly is! Nothing could buy the rich experience of having lunch with a miracle.

If you find nothing to do on a rainy afternoon - or on a sunny one, for that matter - come by and visit with us and you can have lunch with a miracle! I BELIEVE IN MIRACLES. . .I AM ONE!

CHAPTER 37

THE "TESTIMONY MEETING"

In my childhood days of belonging to the fundamentalist church, they had a Wednesday night prayer and testimony meeting. I resented this meeting especially, not because the idea wasn't a good one, but because it did not give what the name of the meeting promised. The prayers were the usual set of instructions to Almighty God to correct all those mistaken folks in other denominations, but the "testimonies" were the greatest spiritual misconduct I ever heard. They were about as confusing as a church cocktail party! They fell into two groups. One group was the young people with slick, quick, memorized recitations week after week. I used to memorize all of them and recite silently with them to amuse myself. The other group was the older folks who gave a complete account of the week's trials and tribulations, pitifully asking for prayer at the end of the routine. It was a game of "can-you-top-this" with life's problems, each one trying to outdo the other with Christian cliff-hanging.

I heard all this and wondered just which side they were on! If they were witnessing for our Lord, they gave a poor witness - the image of a very weak Jesus Christ who wasn't doing much in their lives toward overcoming.

Let me blot out the whole remembrance of that with a WHAM BANG TESTIMONY for our Lord right here! I am a Christian! I am a delighted Christian! I never had it so good! Life is a ball! It is a fantastic adventure I wouldn't miss for anything!

A personal experience with Jesus Christ is not the absence of problems! IT IS THE SOLUTION TO PROBLEMS! My whole world has turned upside down and gone in a new direction! I couldn't be happier about it! I am at last a REAL PERSON! Because JESUS CHRIST IS A REAL PERSON TO ME, there is rich experience. There is never a dull moment! I am excited, and I stay excited!

Christianity is not all black and gray! It is red, white and blue, purple, orange, pink, and yellow!

A child once did a poster which said, "If God doesn't fizz, then why do I feel so bubbly inside?" That's me! Life is not a chronicle of hard times. It is a chronicle of hard times overcome by the power of the Holy Spirit in the lives of ordinary human beings! Like me!

Deliverance is real! Happiness is real! Healing is real! Above all, LIVING FOR JESUS IS REAL!

Years ago, the Ford Motor Company had a slogan for the repair of their products by authorized dealers. It said, "Take your Ford home." I use the same reasoning with my body, mind, and soul. God is my Creator. So, when any part of me gets in need of repair, I take it back home to its Creator. It never fails! Nothing is impossible for God.

My life is jam-packed, and there isn't room for all the exciting things which come my way! I am not hanging on any cliff waiting for the Lord to come rescue me. I HAVE A SPIRITUAL HELICOPTER AND NEVER GET NEAR ANY CLIFF HANGING!

Johnny Mercer, the pop songwriter, wrote a little song in the late forties which chanted, "YOU GOTTA' ACCENTUATE THE POSITIVE, ELIMINATE THE NEGATIVE, DON'T MESS WITH MISTER IN-BETWEEN!" Mr. Mercer didn't know it, but this is the basic theme of my Christianity and ALL CHRISTIANITY WHICH HAS MEANING AND REALITY!

Let me wham home one thought for all of you, and never forget it - CHRISTIANITY SWINGETH!

I BELIEVE IN MIRACLES - I AM ONE!

Bob Murphy is the most delightful drunk in the world! And he's constantly in that state! Whether it's late at night, or early in the morning, he's always high, but in a different way than he used to be. What he's been imbibing for a decade is the best wine in the world, because it's the *New* wine! It's the wine that *can* and *does* change lives, even of people who never were alcoholics.

The problems of an alcoholic are no different than the problems of any individual involved in sin. They may have different names, but the end results are exactly the same, and the withdrawal symptoms from sin of any kind are as traumatic and yet as exciting as those of the alcoholic.

This book will speak to every person in the world! In one way or another, it will touch you, and might even prick you in a way you don't like, but it will do so in a way to make *You* want to change your life style, whether it's drinking, eating or criticizing those who do!

Christianity Rubs Holes in my Religion is bound to rub off on everyone who reads it!

Hunter Ministries Publishing Company
1600 Townhurst
Houston, Texas 77043
Printed in USA.